Inevitable

Nicole Skillen

She had always been inevitable to me no matter how hard I tried to stay away, everything always came back to her. She was the love of my life, the reason for my existence, at least I thought she was.

I guess things change.

CHAPTER ONE

To tell a story I always think you need to go back to the beginning, back to the first moment it all began. That is the only way a true picture can be created.

It was the 20th June 2010, my birthday. The night my life changed and my eyes were truly opened. I was 21 years old; some would say my life was just starting. I was now of a legal age to drink, I could gamble if I felt so inclined, although I never was much of a gambler. I saw what that did to my father when I was younger and it put me off for life.

My name is Kacy Sullivan. I live in Raleigh, North Carolina, although I haven't lived here my whole life. I was born and raised in Hyde County. With a population of around 6,000 you can imagine how close knit the community was. My mum used to say you could simply change the colour of your hair and the whole county would know about it the next day. She wasn't exaggerating either. Living in a small community like Hyde was sometimes a good thing; it meant everybody looked out for each other, but it also meant that nothing was ever a secret. If you wanted every single minor detail of your life known by everyone then that was the place to live.

We left when I was nine years old. My dad got offered a job in Raleigh as a big time architect and the money was just too good to turn down, so here we are twelve years later. I still live with my mum and dad and my baby brother. He's actually almost seventeen now and around 6"2 but I still see him as the adorable little three year old who used to follow me around everywhere.

I don't miss Hyde. I was only nine so I think I was more excited to move somewhere new, to have a new bedroom and new friends. Plus my Aunt Veronica lived in Raleigh and had done for most of my life. She was my favourite person, second to my mum of course, things were always better when she was around, much to her disappointment she'd never been able to have children of her own so to her I was not just a niece, but also a daughter.

Raleigh was a big change from little old Hyde County. It was a big city, the 42nd most populous in the whole of the United States. 423,000 filled the streets of Raleigh and I quickly grew to love the city. We lived near to the city centre in a suburban town called Willow Springs. Dad's company recommended the area because they themselves built it. Lucky for us, we had the pick of a number of large five bedroom houses, several with swimming pools and long gated driveways, as you can imagine, Willow Springs was suddenly a very exciting place for me at the age of nine.

To move from a three bedroom semi-detached house to a beautiful five bedroom mansion, I felt like I was dreaming; my bedroom was twice the size of my old one with built-in wardrobes, a king-size bed and a giant television, I felt like a queen. We had really landed on our feet, as my mum would often say.

I quickly made friends in Raleigh, I went to Magellan Charter Middle School and onto Raleigh Charter High School after that. Like any normal teenager I had my ups and downs all through high school, but I made it my aim to not fall into a cliché and be seen as the prom queen or the geek or the jock. I was simply Kacy.

I had a close group of friends, both boys and girls and we stuck together through high school and even onto college. I met my best friend Whitney Sawyer at Middle School. She had a tangled mess of fire-red hair and glasses. She was so sweet and smart, she would typically be seen as a geek, though to me she was anything but. You wouldn't believe that today she was probably the most beautiful person in the whole city. She had been scouted so many times to do modelling jobs and advertisements, every single time she turned them down because she was studying hard to be a lawyer.

We both agreed to go to North Carolina State University after high school neither of us were particularly keen on the idea of moving across the country, I liked my life in Raleigh. I loved being close to my friends and my family, so although I had offers from the likes of Duke and Yale, NCSU was always the first choice for me.

I studied Architectural Design like my father did, and his brother also. It was something that ran in the family I guess, but I had taken an interest in it since I could remember. My father would take me on site with him; he'd show me plans for new buildings and models of what they would look like.

It always seemed like such an exciting job, to design a building on paper and then watch it develop into the real thing, I imagine it gives you such a sense of achievement. I used to see the glow on my dad's face when he would tell us all about the different buildings he had designed. He still does it today and one day I imagine I'll do the same.

University was an amazing experience. Don't get me wrong, it was difficult, so many late nights and weekends studying at home or in the library. At the age of 21 though, to be less than three months away from graduating with a degree in Architectural Design was a dream come true.

My birthday was a Saturday that year, which fell perfectly considering all the plans I had for that weekend. Just like any other day, I woke at around 8 am to find the sun peeking through my thick crimson blackout curtains. Drawing back the curtains every day to see the view across Willow Springs was still so breath-taking. I had the best view in the house. Moving in day consisted of a three hour stand-off with both my parents to make sure I got the biggest room in the house. I was one step away from chaining myself to the radiator until they gave up. I guess you could say I was a handful when I was younger; I knew what I wanted and just how to get it. I could see just about every part of the town, including the skyline of Raleigh. Our house was built on slightly higher ground than others on the estate so at sunrise and sunset it was truly amazing.

My phone flashed every few minutes with another happy birthday message or Facebook notification. After the first five I had switched it to silent. The incessant beeping of Apple's generic ringtones was rather irritating after a while.

I found it amusing how even people you hardly knew would be among the first to wish you a happy birthday or send you a private message asking 'how's your day going?' It's almost like being a celebrity for the day. Just call me Angelina Jolie. One message in particular caught my eye. A message from Lara.

What can I say about Lara Manning? She was incredibly beautiful. She had long, flowing blonde hair and piercing green eyes and a smile that could light up a room. We had dated for a while in the first year of college and a part of me thought it could have really gone somewhere, but as time went on we grew apart and the spark faded. Ever since we hadn't really been close. We bumped into each other in college or exchanged the occasional text message, but nothing had happened for a while now.

The text read;

From: Lara C

Happy 21st Birthday Kacy,

I hope you have a fantastic day. It will be nice to see you tonight at Flex. Let me know if you're coming,

I miss you :)

L x

Flex was an LGBT Nightclub in Raleigh, I had been several times with friends. Usually, if we went on a night out it would be the first place to go before you'd head to the bigger clubs like Fifteen and Icon. I hadn't heard from Lara in over a month, but it didn't change anything between us; there was never any awkwardness. I was always happy to see her. When we split, the mutual agreement was that there would be no hard feelings between us. Besides we had a lot of mutual friends so it was inevitable that we would run into each other, there was no need for things to be weird.

The thought that she missed me was comforting. It made me smile to know she was still thinking about me. I am only human after all, I hadn't been with anyone in around three months so if something was to happen between me and Lara, I thought to myself what's the harm in that? Besides she was....well let's just say she was *hot;* yes she was undoubtedly hot.

The texts continued throughout the morning; birthday wishes and excited messages from my best friends for the night ahead. Just like every other birthday I had ever had, I came downstairs to find my mum, dad and brother eagerly waiting in the kitchen to present me with cards and gifts and my favourite chocolate pancakes with strawberries and cream, the perfect birthday breakfast. We always made a huge effort in our house whenever it was anyone's birthday. The fact that it was my 21st made today even more special. For months, my mum and dad had been planning my surprise present and I had absolutely no idea what it could be.

Don't get me wrong, I could have done some digging and found out, like my brother always did, but I thought why ruin the surprise, he always said he didn't like surprises, but you could see the slight disappointment in his face when he found out prematurely what he was getting. That was Jason for you, my impatient and stubborn little brother. He would never change.

"Good morning sweetie," chirped my mother from

across the room. She looked her usual glamorous self in a figure hugging plain black dress accessorised with sparkling diamond earrings and a huge choker necklace, I honestly thought sometimes she was ready to go on a night out. She had been a model in her younger days so had always made an effort to look her best and keep up with the latest trends, often asking my opinion on what a 40 something year old should be wearing these days, bearing in mind she was in fact 52 now.

"Happy Birthday Sweetheart. I can't believe my little girl is all grown up." said my dad.

He squeezed me so tight I could barely breathe. I always had been a daddy's girl. He too was dressed and ready for work in his ridiculously overpriced suit. He was 53 a month before my 21^{st,} but he looked great for his age, often passing for a 40 year old. Slightly balding at the front now, but he still had his permanently dyed jet black hair and slim figure from his frequent visits to the gym. I loved my dad so much. He was the softer of my parents. I smiled at them both as the third and final figure came towards me.

"Happy birthday sis. God you're getting old."

Jason laughed and gave his usual cheeky wink. He always did like to wind me up. We had that kind of relationship were one minute we would be screaming at each other and the next we would be best friends again, but he always had my back and I had his no matter what.

"Thanks so much guys…..mmm those pancakes smell delicious, Mum."

She was without a doubt the best cook I'd ever experienced, even better than the many restaurants I had dined in.

"All for you sweetie, but before we have breakfast we can't wait any longer...do you want to see your surprise?"

It was nice to see my mum so excited. She always got giddy whenever she had a surprise for one of us. It was what she lived for.

"Oh yes please, please, please. I can't wait." My parents both beamed at one another. My mum led the way, Dad covered my eyes with his hands, wanting the surprise to remain that way until the very last minute. I had lived in this house for twelve years, but I had no idea as to where I was being lead. My father's hands kept me from seeing anything.

"Almost there sweetheart, keep your eyes closed......hold on......just a second.....okay open them."

When my eyes opened I was stood in the garage looking at what had to be the most beautiful car I had ever seen, plastered across the bonnet was a huge red bow and a banner in the background hanging from the garage ceiling read "Happy Birthday Sweetheart". I couldn't contain my excitement, I passed my driving test two years ago, but had always used my mum's car if I needed to go anywhere. I realised after a minute of staring at pure perfection I hadn't even thanked them yet.

"Omg it's gorgeous. Thank you so, so much. I can't believe you got me a car." I squealed.

"It's a 2.0ltr TDI Volkswagen Scirrocco in your favourite colour of course sweetie. It's got custom made seats and alloys, it has a built in satnav and best of all....it's all yours."

My dad loved cars, he knew my favourite car colour was white. He himself had chosen a white Range Rover last year because I had insisted on the colour. I couldn't believe I had my very own car, I was speechless it literally was a dream come true and the best birthday present I could have ever wished for.

The rest of the morning and afternoon consisted of me thanking my family over and over again, for all the amazing gifts I had been given. Not only had I gotten a car, but my mum had bought me a new apple mac laptop. To be completely honest it was needed more than anything. I was never off my laptop, it was so over used I almost felt sorry for it.

My brother had saved up his summer job money to buy me a gorgeous Michael Kors watch. The new summer addition all in rose gold. My Grandma and Grandad had given me the trust fund they had saved up for me all these years. Every week for 21 years of my life they had put five pounds into a private bank account. They did the same with my parents before me and they are currently doing the same with Jason. I had an amazing five thousand and five hundred pound to spend on whatever I wished. The amount of clothes I could buy with that money or the holidays I could go on, the possibilities really were endless.

My 21ˢᵗ birthday was the beginning of the rest of my life, I felt on top of the world.

There was always something magical about birthdays, a day when everyone comes together to celebrate one person. It was something I always looked forward to, even more than Christmas.

It wasn't just about the presents or the money it was about celebrating with family and friends. My 21ˢᵗ was probably the only day in my whole entire life that my family and friends were together in the same room; laughing and drinking and generally enjoying life. To me that was the most important thing. They are the memories that you carry with you forever.

I spent most of the day shopping at the mall with Whitney, she was as excited as I was about my new car. She took the bus to college with me almost every day so the prospect of us now driving was a huge deal.

I had to buy a new outfit for the party later that evening. I must have been in around ten different shops before I found the perfect dress. I wasn't one for wearing dresses all the time unless it was a big occasion, like tonight.

My style you could say was trendy, but girly if I was to be labelled, I guess that's what we would call here in North Carolina, a Lipstick Lesbian.

My everyday style was simple. A pair of skinny jeans, converse and a plain tee. I wasn't the type to be stomping around college in a 10inch pair of high heels, a mini skirt and a top so low cut pretty much everybody could see your assets.

If there was one thing everyone knew about me, it was that I liked to be comfortable.

The dress I had found came with a hefty price tag of $300, usually I would spend around $50, but my birthday money was burning a hole in my pocket already. After all I would only be twenty one once.

After buying a new bag, matching shoes, two new pairs of converse, a pair of skinny jeans, and several new tops the bill came to around $700, now that was a shopping spree.

We made one last pit stop to Starbucks for an Iced Mocha. Literally the best drink anyone, anywhere, will ever have. With that being said, my favourite drink fresh in one hand, it was time to head home.

The party would be starting around 7 pm. I myself had suggested having it at home months ago instead of hiring a venue.

We had a big enough house to accommodate and a back garden that would put a sculpture park to shame. My mum had recently bought a brand new set of rattan furniture for our ever overpopulating garden, so why not put it to good use. A caterer was hired, and a local DJ set up in the backyard. The house was trimmed up full of old embarrassing photos, one of my Goth phase, another of my tomboy phase and more than one of my Barbie cheerleader phase. I would later punish my mother for those. Everyone knew where I lived, it was easy access for all my family and friends. So home had seemed like the perfect place to host my party.

People started to arrive around 6 pm. I was slightly behind schedule as my mum constantly reminded me, every five seconds.

"Sweetheart you need to hurry, your guests are arriving." I could tell from her tone of voice she wasn't liking the idea of having to entertain them herself, so the quicker I got ready the better for everyone involved. "Two minutes mom. I'm just finishing my hair." Okay so that was the third time I had said that, but my hair was difficult to tackle some days and today was one of those days. Why is it when you're out to impress nothing ever goes right? Sods law I say.

I knew it would be most of my family arriving early because my friends were very much like me, they would be fashionably late without a doubt.

The party went like any other I guess, my friends and family took it in turns to tell embarrassing stories about me, we all had a giggle at the photos around the house and everyone enjoyed the food on offer. I was showered with even more cards and gifts. I remember the six foot long dining room table they were laid upon being fully covered.

"Wow birthday girl. Who knew you were so popular?" That was my best friend's voice, extremely noticeable. She pulled me in for a hug whilst blatantly pointing towards the large present to the right of the table. It was wrapped beautifully in my favourite colours, orange and white. A huge orange bow decorated the front perfectly. "That one's from me, but you can't open it until tomorrow. I want to see your face."

"Wow I'm intrigued, I hope you're not getting me back for my empty box trick last year." I gave her a quick smirk.

"Would I ever? I did think about it for a second actually then I thought...well I'm just not that cruel."

"Very funny, you loved it. By the way I so don't believe you wrapped that yourself."

"I so did!!" the grin on her face said otherwise.

"Seriously, you made me wrap all your Christmas presents for you last year because yours looked like a child had been let loose with some sticky tape and glitter."

We both laughed hysterically because she knew herself how true that was. Whitney was good at a lot of things, but she terrible at wrapping.

"Okay smart ass, so I didn't wrap it myself, but I watched some really good looking guy wrap it for me instead. I'm thinking I might save you a job this year and go back to get all my Christmas presents done."

She was hilarious, the things she would do to get a guy's attention was beyond what any reasonably sane person would do, I had to love her for it though.

"Oh great. I sure hope he doesn't quit before the year is out then, that will save me a good few hours."

"Let's hope not! Anyway is it time to go yet? I'm so excited."

"I can tell, you're like a new born puppy." I laughed and pushed her towards the crowded living room.

"I need to do some more mingling, so you my beautiful best friend need to occupy your time." I shouted after her as I left the room giggling to myself "Try not to pee on anything." It took her a few seconds before she realised I was referencing the puppy dog statement, in return I got the middle finger.

Everyone started to leave around 10:30 pm but for me and my friends the party was only just beginning. The clubs in Raleigh were the next stop and if you asked me at that moment in time was I excited? That would have been the understatement of the century.

Me, Whitney, Jessica and Lauren all jumped into my father's car. My other friends Jake, Brooke, Ryan and Chloe jumped in with my Mum. Neither of them liked to drink a lot of alcohol, one glass of White Wine or a Jack Daniels would usually be the extent of it. So both my parents were adamant on making sure we had a safe trip into town.

Saturday the 20th June had been pencilled in on the calendar for a long time. All of us had saved every last penny and eagerly awaited a night out to never forget. We could go out whenever we wanted, every single weekend if we chose to do so, but the night of my 21st was different, because money wasn't a factor.

We had already purchased wristbands and paid for VIP seating in the best clubs. Champagne was even on tap, kindly purchased by my parents.

I was the youngest out of my group of friends, they were twenty two and twenty three. Then there was me,

Whitney and Brooke that shared the same age. They had only recently turned twenty one in the past few months so I wasn't the baby by far.

My 21st was set up to be the best night out I'd ever experienced. I required no more fake ID's, no more under twenty one party's and no more illegal drinking. I was now at an age were the world was my oyster, time to start living it, finally.

The main reason June 20th 2010 was the best night out ever was not simply because of the things I stated above, but because it was the night I met her. The night I saw the bigger picture, I saw outside of my life in Willow Springs and my life at NCSU. I saw into the future and the possibility's it could bring.

The night was beyond amazing, first we went to Flex. I felt like a star. We had VIP queue jumping passes and a special seated VIP area was reserved just for me and all my friends. There was about thirteen of us all together, but by the time we moved onto Club Fifteen shortly after midnight, there was over twenty five people in our VIP box, give or take a few. Several of my friends had gotten rather giddy as the night progressed, dragging random people into the cordoned off area. Whitney especially, she was newly single, so you couldn't blame her for the four obviously hansom guys she had invited over. I was excited to see how she'd get out of that one, with all four of them vying for her attention.

Between 1 pm and 2 pm Fifteen was the place to be. That's when it really started to get busy. The queue to get in was over forty people long by this time, some had been queuing for an hour already. The chances of getting in were slim to none because not a lot of people wanted to leave once inside. Luckily for us, we had planned this evening for a long time. Much to the envy of everyone stood in line we placed our queue jumping passes in the hands of the bouncer. It took no longer than twenty seconds for us to be inside.

Club Fifteen was such an amazing place, it had been renovated a while back to look like something right out of New York City. Inside the hardwood flooring was solid oak, plush red carpets covered the walkways giving you the feeling you were on the red carpet at the Grammy's. The gentleman stood by the entrance with state of the art cameras added to the effect. The type of cameras that don't add ten pounds instead they make you look like Americas next top model. Finally it was the lighting that sealed the deal. Dark, seductive and sensual across all three floors. I couldn't get enough of the place.

There were three different bars, one of them just for cocktails, several dance floors each with a different theme and DJ. Best of all if you were to head right to the top floor, balconies overlooked the whole of Raleigh. Not only was the view amazing, but throw in a few palm trees, a gorgeous seating area and a bartender on hand. That gave you one thing, the most beautiful place to relax and drink in the whole of the city. I had the privilege of being on that top floor overlooking the whole of the city with the people I loved. My best friends in the whole world and I couldn't have asked for anything more that evening.

What I was about to experience was a bonus like no other.

CHAPTER TWO

I saw her in the corner of my eye, I was stood at the bar ordering what had to be my third sex on the beach Cocktail. I couldn't get enough of those things.
The bartender also tried flirting with me for the third time that evening, not wanting to get into the whole, I'm gay conversation. Instead I just smiled politely and paid for my drink.
I don't know what made me look twice in her direction, maybe it was the sound of her laugh that caught my attention, but something inside me wanted to look over again and when I did I couldn't look away.
First I saw her eyes, they were such a powerful blue that even little me stood half way across the room was

mesmerised by them. Her loosely curled brown hair fell just above her shoulders and her teeth were so clear to see when she laughed. They were perfect in every way, the kind of teeth you expect a superstar to own. She had olive skin and a slim, toned body. It could be seen perfectly through her grey, ripped, skinny jeans and the tight, white, t-shirt she wore under her leather jacket. At first I couldn't work out if she was gay or not, but then she looked back at me. Clearly, I must have been making it obvious that I was staring at her, but she didn't look away, I followed her eyes as she took in every inch of me. My hair, my dress, my drink. She eyed every part of me with a small smile on her face and then she whispered in her friend's ear before starting towards me.

I honestly didn't know what to do or what to say, was she going to ask me why I was staring at her? What would I say? I turned away, back towards the bar before she got to me. In that moment the only thought I could fathom was how much I needed a mirror so I could check my make-up, my hair and my teeth. There was nothing worse than talking to someone you found attractive, then realising afterwards you had something stuck in your teeth. Trust me I'm speaking from experience.
"Hey, I'm Alex……you are?"
There was a slight pause on my behalf. I must have looked like a complete idiot. Pauses in films were okay, they added to the effect, but in real life you just looked

ridiculous. I could only imagine what her first impressions of me really were. I took her in for a minute as she spoke to me, she was even more gorgeous up close. Her voice was so husky and seductive. She had a confidence and charisma that radiated from every part of her.

"Hi, I'm Kacy."

I couldn't think of anything witty or smart to say, I was a confident person myself, but I couldn't even think of what to say in front of this girl, so being confident and charismatic like her just wasn't an option right then. I had to keep it together.

"I like that name, nice to meet you Kacy. I saw you earlier buying one of those cocktails, they must be good?"

That made me feel slightly better, knowing she had seen me, before I had seen her. Maybe she too had been watching me that evening.

"Yes, they're my favourite, can I get you one? You won't regret it." I said.

"I already have a drink at my table, but maybe next time? Is it your birthday today?"

"Yes, how did you know?" I was mesmerized by everything she said, I just wanted to keep her talking for as long as I could. Everything she said was so intense, the heat between us was undeniable.

"You were the girl stood in the middle of all those people over there, when they sang happy birthday to you? Also the big badge attached to your bag kind of gives it away." She said this with a smirk on her face, she obviously found that amusing. I'd forgotten about the gigantic badge Whitney had made me wear. It had to remain on some part of my attire that evening, those were the rules. The fact that I had gone very red and embarrassed, when all my friends decided to sing to me, was clearly something else she had seen that evening.

"Yes unfortunately that was me. My friends like to show me up. I see you found that amusing."

"Very....so Kacy I really should get back over to my friends. I don't want to seem to forward, but can I see you again sometime?"

She was leant up against the bar, looking directly into my eyes when she spoke to me. This girl gave me butterflies with every word that formed from her perfect lips. I really didn't want her to leave, it was something I couldn't control.

"Sure, I'd really like that. Are you leaving? Or do you and your friends want to come upstairs to the balcony?"

I was hoping with every inch of me she would say yes. I had known this girl for five minutes, but it felt like so much longer. The connection between us was electrifying.

"If I come up to the balcony with you, you have to promise me one thing?" she said with a little smile that made the side of her mouth curl up in such a sexy way.

"What would that be?" I said. Trying my best to be just as sexy as her. Although I think the chances of that happening were very slim.

"You have to promise that after tonight's over I get to take you somewhere for breakfast? I know the perfect place."

How could I say no to that? At that moment in time she could have taken me anywhere she wanted. I really don't think I would have questioned it.

"I would really love that, breakfast sounds great."

The smile on my face was pretty obvious, but I had the feeling she often had this effect on woman. I don't think it was exactly new to her.

Alex strolled back to her table to tell her friends she would be leaving them. I did offer for her friends to come, but she said they preferred to be down on the middle floor. That's where the DJ played base music. I introduced her to a few of my friends once we reached the balcony.

"Alex this is Whitney, my best friend and this is Lauren. Guys this is Alex." Everyone was so polite when I introduced them to Alex, each in turn giving their own glare or wink as if to say well done with that one. Whitney pulled me to one side to whisper in my ear when she got the chance.

"Wow Kacy, you came back with the hottest lesbo chick I've ever seen, besides yourself of course. I think you've out done me this evening with that one. I'm definitely being the best woman at your wedding."

She squeezed my arm before running off to join her entourage of men. Well, it looked like Alex had the approval of pretty much everyone in the room.

I wanted to get to know her better, so we went to the far corner of the balcony away from prying eyes. I know it was my birthday and all my friends were there for me, but I had to get to know her, besides half of my friends had already hooked up. All my focus and attention from that moment on was occupied for the rest of the evening.

We talked for over an hour about anything and everything. I found out so much about her. Her full name was Alex Lorena Dawson, the middle name being given to her in remembrance of her great grandmother, which she was quick to point out. I thought it was nice.

She was 23 years old and had never attended College. Instead she had gotten a job in her Mum and Dads bar straight out of school. A bar in which she now owned with her sister Natalie, she informed me that her parents had passed away in a tragic car accident two years earlier. I was shocked to hear this and didn't really know what to say, other than the usual I am so sorry to hear that. I didn't feel uncomfortable though, by her ease of speaking about it I think she had come to terms with everything, as hard as that must be. She had learned to live life to the full after that because you never know how short your time may be.

Alex had lived in Raleigh her whole life, but had intentions to travel the world and maybe even open a bar abroad, if she could choose it would've been somewhere in the Caribbean. Everything about her was fascinating, the way she told a story drew me in from the first word.

We talked about everything from school, to me wanting to be an architect, to past relationships. We got onto family, friends and dream holiday destinations. It was 3 am before we knew it and the club was beginning to close. I had completely sobered up after talking to her for almost two hours, I hadn't even thought about getting another drink. My friends had dropped one by one until the last two remaining were Brooke and Jake, the cutest couple I knew. They had been together for three years and always relished a good night out. They eventually said their final goodbyes.

"So are you ready for breakfast?" Said Alex.

"What like right now? It's three o'clock? Who serves breakfast at three o'clock?"

I was confused I thought she meant she wanted to go for breakfast the next day, at least when I had gone home, slept and changed. The girl was fascinating.

"Yes like right now. The best time to go for breakfast is after a night out. You have no idea how hungry alcohol makes me. I'm going to take you to a place that does the best pancakes in the whole of North Carolina."

Well I wasn't exactly going to say no to the offer, not a single bone in my body was tired, something about being with her made me feel so alive. The diner Alex took me to was a ten minute walk away from Club Fifteen. It was named Early Bird Diner and it opened at 3 am every single day. The only people in there at that time in the morning were truckers, making a pit stop before hitting the road again and the occasional strollers from a long night out, like me and Alex. The diner was slightly hidden away, it wasn't something I'd ever come across before, but then again I never really went into downtown Raleigh, other than for a night out. She swore by this place, she guaranteed they would be the best pancakes I'd ever tasted. She wasn't wrong.

"I've ordered us both chocolate chip pancakes with maple syrup, vanilla whipped cream and strawberries on the side. Trust me you will love them."

She was very confident on the fact I would love these pancakes, I liked that about her.

"How did you know what to order? There is an endless menu and you choose probably my favourite pancakes ever. Actually I had them for breakfast this morning." I licked the last bit of syrup and cream off the fork. The grin on my face must have been wider than a Cheshire cat.

"I swear by these pancakes and that one is my favourite so I figured you'd like it too, you'd have to be crazy not to." She winked.

"Well I like your taste in food." It was brief and not at all a flirty response to the wink she had given, I was so lame.

"Most people grab a takeaway when they head home after a night out, but having breakfast at a pancake diner might just be my new favourite thing to do." Especially in present company, I left that part out.

"I guess I'm not most people, I like to try new things. Eating pancakes early hours in the morning happened to be one of the things I became quite accustomed to. I'm so glad you like it."

"I've really enjoyed tonight Alex, thank you for bringing me here." I said.

"I have too, I can walk you home if you like? The sun will be rising shortly and that's the best part." I could see the twinkle in her eye, she didn't want this night to end and to be completely honest, neither did I.

"If you are planning on walking me home, it might take a while, I Live in Willow Springs."

To walk from Downtown Raleigh to Willow Springs, it would probably take a solid two hours. We had arranged a mini bus to pick us up from outside ICON, but that was at 4 am. It was supposed to be taking me, Whitney and Brooke back to my house, but it was now 5 am and I was with Alex, not with Whitney. My way of getting home was no longer available. I could always ring my mum, she wouldn't be overly happy about me disturbing her beauty sleep, but I was her only daughter I'm sure she would get over it. That's when Alex suggested something I found just too irresistible to turn down.

"You could come back to mine then? I only live around the corner from here. You can crash until later today and when I've slept off the alcohol, I can take you home."

How could I turn that down? I mean she wasn't asking me to go back for sex, although if she made a move would I really have turned it down? Definitely not.

I wasn't the type of girl to go home with someone after a night out. If I was seeing someone I felt it was always appropriate to wait until at least, the third or fourth date.

"That sounds great. If you don't mind." I smiled my best smile and she returned hers. "Not at all." We strolled towards her apartment, taking our time. I was keen to take in the surroundings, having never been to her neighbourhood before. We passed her bar along the way, it was called Dawson's Grill & Bar. It served food during the day and served as a bar at night. I was sure I'd seen it before in passing but never had I been inside. I heard people talk about it at work once, as the new place to go before you hit the nightclubs. I thought to myself, I would be trying it out from now on.

"I'll show you inside sometime, we had it refurbished late last year so it's got a whole new vibe to it. I think you'd really like it."

If you're there I think I would definitely like it, obviously I didn't say that out loud, but you can't blame me for thinking it.

We arrived at her apartment after walking for just over five minutes and it really was beautiful. She told me that when her parents died, both her and her sister sold the family home outside of Raleigh. They bought two apartments in the downtown area so they could be closer to the bar and to their grandparents. As you could imagine they were really struggling after the death of their daughter.

Alex's apartment was on the top floor, it had an amazing open plan living room with brick walls and a solid wood kitchen. It had two huge bedrooms with built in wardrobes and king-size beds. She had a sofa big enough to fit ten people comfortably, but by far the best part was the full length, ceiling to floor glass windows. They opened out onto a rooftop decking area with some amazing views of the city.

I couldn't believe it, the views that I loved so much on Club Fifteens balcony, the ones I had bragged about earlier that evening for over ten minutes, she had them right there, in her own apartment. Actually the views in her apartment were ten times better. The apartment was considerably higher up than the top floor of Fifteen, so the views from up there were absolutely breath-taking. She had I think the most gorgeous apartment I had ever seen.

"I can't believe you let me rant on for ages about the view from the balcony, at the club, when you have this amazing view right here!"

I was still taking everything in at this point. She laughed to herself for a minute before saying,

"Well I just liked listening to you talk, several times tonight you have described a view or a building and the way you talk about them, it's fascinating to me. I mean, I just see them as buildings, I don't look as deep into it as you do. I can tell you're going to be a fantastic architect, you have such a passion for this stuff."

She winked at me before twirling and heading for the kitchen.

"Do you want a drink?"

"I'd love some water please, my mouth is so dry."

"No problem, filtered okay? I have no bottles left I'm afraid."

"Tap water is fine with me honest, I'm not posh."

She laughed to herself, entering the lounge area two minutes later with an ice cold glass of water.

Those pancakes had really done a number on my mouth, I was dying for a nice cold drink. She handed me the glass of water and ushered me out onto the balcony.

"Sunrise will be in about five minutes and it's the best thing you will ever experience from up here, I promise you. If I ever need any sort of inspiration I sit exactly here, at around this time, first thing on a morning and just watch the world wake up to begin another day."

"You are aware that it's the second time you have introduced me to one of the best things I will ever experience? Twice in one night, you're giving yourself a lot to live up to here."

"And the nights not even over yet." I couldn't help but bare the most ridiculous smile across my face, she must of known from the get go that I liked her, the beaming grin was a bit of a give-away.

She was so at ease, just sat waiting and watching and so was I. This amazing girl who I had known for only five hours was everything I could have ever wanted.

We both sat in silence as the sun came up and neither of

us needed to speak, she placed her hand on mine and our eye contact said it all. This wasn't the awkward silence you would get on a first date, when you'd ran out of things to say. This was utter perfection, there was no small exchanges of chitter chatter just to fill the air, there was no need for entertainment to cure any sort of boredom, there simply was no boredom. The feeling I had right in that moment, as I looked into her eyes and the sun came up, was so intense, so passionate, I felt as though I had known her my whole life. At that moment she kissed me, her lips fit perfectly with mine. I closed my eyes and fell deeply into a kiss that would change my life. I did in fact miss most of the sunrise, not that I was complaining.

The kisses became harder and more intense, the passion and the tension between us was something I had never experienced. It was inevitable what would follow, but it wouldn't just be a one night stand, it wouldn't be just sex. It would be magical, I knew that before it happened. I could feel it with every bone in my body. The way she kissed my neck and touched my body was growing more electrifying with every movement.
I had never felt so attractive, so wanted and needed the way she made me feel in that moment. The way she yearned for my body and hungered for my touch, just as I did for her. The night finally came to a close at around 8 am, when we both fell to sleep in each other's arms.
I could honestly say at that moment in time I felt so

relaxed and so at peace with everything.

I had travelled a road for so many years and finally reached my destination. I had found what most people search for their entire life. She was right earlier on, I had just experienced the third best thing since meeting her. I knew my friends would think I was crazy, who can feel that way after knowing someone for eight hours. It's not something I could explain to them, it's only something I felt at that time.

People want to believe in love at first sight, they want to believe in epic love story's that begin and end like the movies, but that's not always the case. I don't believe you can love someone as soon as you lay eyes upon them.

I could tell you that the moment I met Alex, fireworks spontaneously erupted in the night sky. I could tell you that our eyes locked onto one another's and right then we just knew it was true love.

That however was not the case, but our meeting was one of perfection. We laughed, we smiled and we talked through to sunrise and on after that. Everything between us was undeniably natural, like we had been doing it our whole lives and that to me is as good as it gets. It may not have been love at first sight, but it was desire at first sight, it was attraction and intensity beyond any reasonable doubt, that was clear to see, but love at first sight?

I believe until proven wrong that it is simply a myth created for humankind so that we can believe in a love like no other, but what we had was even better. It was real and it certainly was set in stone to be epic.

CHAPTER THREE

The following days passed by so quick, we spent every spare, waking minute we had together. After that first night she drove me home and I hadn't wanted to leave her, just in case it had all been a dream. A cruel dream that was dangling her perfection in front of me to only take it back and claim it as a nightmare instead.

I still had to attend university to sit my final exams and Alex had her usual work routine, but in between we couldn't stay away from each other.

I looked forward to every sunset, eagerly awaiting a new day and every sunrise, knowing that I would soon see her again. She was like a book I never wanted to put down, a best seller with torn pages and coffee stains.

I wanted to keep reading, delving in deeper to find out every last detail about who she was. I wanted to discover the countless adventures and experiences she had once been a part of. She slowly became my addiction.

Over a month passed like this, I spent most nights at Alex's apartment. We lay awake all night talking about anything and everything, watching the sunset became a part of our daily routine.

Most of it was a complete blur when I look back, we did nothing of significance yet everything of worth. The memories of lying with her, kissing her, breathing in her every breath were memories that would forever be embedded in my soul.

After a few weeks my mum had told me,

"You too will get sick of each other you know, it's always more exciting if you give each other time to miss one another, sweetheart." This being said with a concerned look on her face, but also the hint of a smile hiding in the corners of her mouth. I knew she was happy to see me so happy.

"I've spent every day with you and dad for the past twenty one years of my life, I'm not sick of you guys yet." I gave her my cheekiest smile and she couldn't help but laugh. I knew my mum, I knew she was concerned like any parent would have been, but at the same time she loved to see me happy, that was all her and my father wanted. Some might say me and Alex were moving fast, it didn't feel that way to me, it felt right.

I wasn't the type to jump into a relationship, claiming to love someone after being together for a mere week, that was just unrealistic. I was definitely a realist when it came to relationships. I would always be the first to question my friends if they were moving too fast, or jumping in too deep, talking marriage and kids after a few months was insanity. You can't really know someone until you have been with them for at least three months. I believe that is how long the 'honeymoon' period will last. After that cracks will start to appear, true personalities will come out and you see the person for who they really are.

All that being said I couldn't help but feel I was slowly beginning to break my own rules, was I about to go against my own beliefs?

The summer was so hot that year, averaging 30 degrees every single day. When college was finally out we had nothing to do but enjoy the weather. We took a trip down to Wilmington to explore the gorgeous beaches, they were by far the best across the whole 300 miles of barrier island stretch.

The landscape was magical, people came here just to relax and enjoy the beautiful seafood on offer. This was served in the local bars all day, so fresh from being caught in the early morning.

There was something about being in Wilmington, or being anywhere on the Coast for that matter, all the small unique towns had something to offer. They were all so beautiful in their own little way. Alex's family used to have a beach house down on the coast of Wilmington, between Carolina and Kure beaches. One of two that they owned, her grandparents also owned another over in Oregon.

Unfortunately they had to sell up once her parents passed away as they could no longer afford to keep it. A tear came to her eye as she explained all about the memories she had of that place, so many of her and her sister growing up.

We stayed in a B&B on the coast, just for one night. Our first little trip away together, we had only been seeing each other three weeks at this point, neither of us had spoken about officially being together, although it felt to me like we were.

We lay on the beach that night after dinner, the sun had set and the stars were sparkling in the clear night sky. The met office had unbelievably predicted a meteor shower, which excited us both. I had only ever seen one meteor shower, but I was so young. It's something I think most people are only lucky to see once in their whole life.

"I spoke to my grandma earlier, she said she can't wait to meet you." Alex's grandma was very important to her and Natalie, she was the only family they had left. Their grandfather had died several years ago, so Grandma Rose was everything to Alex.

"I can't wait to meet her too, she sounds so lovely, is she okay?"

"Yes she's fine, Natalie went to the Doctors with her this morning because she's lost her appetite and feels a bit weak lately, but she said it's nothing. They're just going

to do a few checks when she goes back next week."
Alex was always so strong when she spoke about her Grandma, but I knew it concerned her that she was ill. She was 74 now and Alex worried quite a lot about how much longer she would have with her.

"That's good then, did she say anything else?"

"She said I should stop being soft and just ask you to be my girlfriend."

Alex was laid on her back looking at the stars and smiling. I had never met her grandma, but she already liked me because she knew how happy I made Alex. I didn't know how to respond.

"So what are you waiting for?" I winked my best and most seductive wink and she couldn't help but laugh.

"Will you do me the honour of officially being my girlfriend Miss Kaci Sullivan?" She sat up from her position and looked me directly in the eyes, grinning from ear to ear. How could I say no to this gorgeous person?

"Of course I will Miss Alex Dawson, I couldn't think of anything better."

Then she kissed me, suddenly my heart skipped a beat and my stomach exploded with a flurry of butterflies. A tremor ran through my whole body as it did every single time we locked lips this way. It wasn't just a kiss, it was the kind of passionate embrace you would perform, if you knew it would be your last. It was epic in more ways than one.

Sometimes you can't explain what you see in a person, besides the fact that they are beautiful or kind or funny, they are all words you could use to describe anyone, but sometimes it's just the way they seem to take you to a place where no one else can.

That is the way I would describe what I saw in Alex, I only saw her, and everything else was just background.

"Look Al, the shooting stars." I shouted, a little louder than needed seen as half the beach ended up looking our way. The child within me was in awe. What I was witnessing was pure beauty, pure astonishment.

My Grandma always used to tell me if you ever see a shooting star then you should make a wish, it will always come true.

"Make a wish babe." I said to Alex, and her response melted my heart.

"You're my shooting star Kaci, everything I have ever wished for is everything you are."

I was really falling for this girl and how could I not? She always knew the right things to say, she would always put me first and treat me in a way I thought only princesses were treated, she was utter perfection.

I no longer envied the kind of love you saw in the movies, because that was what we had. My life at that point was like a film but without the drama.

I never wanted someone who would promise me the stars and the moon because that would be unrealistic.

I just wanted someone who would promise to lie beneath them with me and watch them shine.

Alex was that someone for me. Laying there underneath the shooting stars, watching as they got bigger and smaller again, each one lighting up the sky in their own unique way. I thought about our loved ones that had passed, I thought about other people all over the world that would be wishing on a star right now. Would they be wishing for health? Or wealth? Or love? Or happiness? Everyone had a wish, a wish that may be their last hope. The thought was so sad, right then I wished that all those people would get what they had wished for.

"My grandma told me something after my parents passed, she said that stars are not just stars in the sky, but rather openings where all our loved ones that have passed on can shine their light down on us, to show they are happy. I like to believe in that, it makes me happy to think that."

"Your grandma is a very wise woman. I think all grandmas are, that is a beautiful thing to believe in Alex, never let that go."

There was always something about a person's grandma, maybe it was the fact they had been around a long time, and they had seen and heard a lot of things.

They had experienced most things in life so they always knew what to say and how to make you feel better, even in your darkest hour.

The meteor shower continued for 30 minutes, they became less frequent after that, so we made our way back to the Bed & Breakfast.

The night away with Alex was perfect, I could not have asked for it to go any better, we were officially together and that made me happier than I had ever been.

A few more weeks passed by, all my exams were done. I now eagerly awaited the results in less than a month's time, to see if I would be following in my dad's footsteps. I had found out the week before that I had an internship spot guaranteed at my dad's company, if I got the right grades of course. I had every faith in myself that I would. I had worked so hard for this for over a year, practically living in the library and burying my head in books, making sure I was prepared for the final semester's exams. I could honestly say I felt confident in the work I had produced.

Alex and I were still inseparable and that's just the way we liked it. She still had a business to run so although my days and nights were freed up for the remainder of the summer, Alex's unfortunately were not. I kept myself busy most of the time, my friends and family were always happy to have me around. I took up yoga with my mum once a week on a Tuesday, I went for dinner with Brooke every Wednesday and I saw Whitney almost every day. She was my best friend after all, we had been best friends for so long, we didn't even ask to meet up anymore, we would just turn up on one another's doorsteps and let ourselves in.

Alex did a lot of day shifts at the bar, but there were some nights she had to work late, mainly to oversee the general running if Natalie wasn't there. Much to my delight they came to an agreement that Alex would work during the day, 5 days a week and 1 night, Sunday being the only day the bar was shut. Natalie would then work the 1 day shift and 5 nights, she much preferred to work the late shift. She had worked in bars since she was eighteen years old, so she liked the liveliness. That suited Alex just fine because she preferred her nights in.

When she was on a late she would always finish at 2 am depending on how busy the bar was of course, last orders was usually 1 am, that's when most of the people cleared out into the nightclubs further up town.

I would always arrive at the bar around 1 am to keep her company whilst she locked up and put the money away. I was always up at that time anyway, I definitely was not the type to be tucked up in bed by 10 pm, the amount of times I had turned in at 3 am and then been up for a class at 6 am was to many to count, looking back I'm surprised I made it through those days.

It was Friday 23rd July and for some reason unknown to me at the time, that night was different. The bar was already closed when I arrived just after midnight. I thought to myself that maybe she had shut up a little early, Friday nights were never as busy as Saturdays, but the lights were out and as I peered through the window I could see nobody inside.

Come to think of it I hadn't had a text off Alex for the past two hours, she usually checked in every hour even when she was really busy, I didn't know what to think. Why had she left early? Why hadn't she told me? Where had she gone? So many questions that I didn't know how to get the answers too. I walked to her apartment, if she wasn't at the bar maybe she had gone home, maybe she wasn't feeling well and her phone had died which is why she hadn't text.

Her apartment was empty when I got there, I knew where the spare key was so I let myself in. I pulled out my cell phone again, still no reply. I tried to call again, still no answer. As I started to panic, I felt hopeless and helpless. So many possibilities ran through my head, had she been abducted, had someone mugged her on her way home, had she been in an accident.

Never once did the thought that she had maybe met someone else that evening and gone home with them cross my mind, many people after only six weeks of dating would probably jump straight to the paranoid conclusion that the person was cheating, but I knew Alex and she wasn't that person, I remember thinking something was really wrong here.

Over an hour of worrying passed, I was almost ready to phone 911 when my phone started to ring out my favourite song, it was Alex calling.

"Oh My God, Alex why haven't you called? Are you okay? I've been so worried."

There was silence on the line for a few seconds as she steadied herself to speak.

"I......I don't......I don't know how to say it...Rose, my grandma, she's got....she's got cancer. I'm sorry I didn't call I rushed straight to the hospital. I need to go, the

doctors are here, I will call you later babe."
I barely had time to mutter I'm sorry before she put the phone down. My heart sank into my stomach, she sounded so unbelievably heart broken and I was completely helpless, there was nothing I could do to make this better.

I had only met Rose the week before and she had to be the loveliest person I'd ever met, such a pleasure to be around and so kind, tentative, and selfless. She had spent her whole life helping others and this is how she was repaid, why it always happened to the best people I do not know. I received a text an hour later explaining in more detail,

From: My Alex

They said she has cancer of the stomach and that it has spread to most of her major organs, that's why she was struggling to eat. The weakness and the stomach pains it's all to do with the cancer. They basically said it's too late and there's nothing they can do, not even a young fighting fit person would survive a cancer as fierce. They have predicted she has 2-3 months left. I don't know what to do, she is everything to me Kacy, a part of me has just died inside. I need to stay with her, Nat is here to. I will call you tomorrow. Goodnight my love.

I couldn't imagine the pain Alex must have been feeling at that moment in time, she had already lost her mother and father a few years before and now to find out the devastating news about her grandma. I felt so heartbroken for her. Nothing I could do would make it any better for her, to sit by and watch someone you care so deeply for suffer was the most heart-breaking of experiences.

The next day my life truly fell apart, everything I thought I knew, everything I felt and hoped for was being questioned.

Alex arrived back to her apartment around three o'clock in the afternoon the following day. I waited there for her, I knew she would return home and I wanted to be there to comfort her as best I could. I remember the drawn look on her face, the sadness in her voice when she spoke and the lack of energy she now possessed. I had never seen her this way, Alex wasn't a sad person she was always happy and smiley and energetic that was what I really adored about her, she was the reason I smiled every single day.

"Hey Al, are you okay babe? I'm sorry that's a stupid question, of course you're not okay."

I didn't know what to say, I didn't know if she wanted me there or if she wanted to be alone, I couldn't read her at that moment. I embraced her tightly not wanting to let go.

"I'm as good as I can be I guess. Did you stay here last night?"

She kicked off her shoes and sat down on the sofa, completely exhausted.

"Yes, I hope that's okay, I wanted to be here for when you got back. Did you stay at the hospital all night?"

I gave her a sympathetic smile, I wanted her to open up to me. She knew she could tell me anything, but I completely understood that it was difficult for her to come to terms with it all.

"Yes, they said we could take her home this morning so Nat is with her now. I said I'd call back in a few hours, I needed to come and speak to you first."

She placed her head in her hands and sighed before she continued, I was worried for what might come next. She looked as though she was about to tell me it was over, my heart stopped.

"I have to go away for a while Kacy. My grandma only has months left and she can't spend them here, she wants to be at her favourite place, down on the coast of Oregon a place called Cannon Beach. She and my granddad used to go there several times a year she hoped one day they would move there together, that's where she wants to spend her last days. I have to give her that wish Kacy, me and Nat both need to do this for her."

She took my hands in hers and looked me directly in the eyes, I saw the pain within them. I saw the tears on the surface ready to pour out at any given moment. She could see I had no response so she continued.

"I don't know what this means for us, I'm sorry. I can't think about that right now, my head is hurting and my heart is aching Kacy. I have no idea what to do, I feel like I'm about to relive my parents death all over again, and I don't think I can cope with that."

I held her in my arms giving her as much support as I could, she was holding me up also after the news that made me feel I would lose her. I felt I wouldn't have been able to stand if I tried.

"Will you lie with me for a few hours?" it was almost a plea that escaped her lips.

"Of course I will Alex, anything you need."

I should have said more, I should have told her that everything would be okay, that it was okay for her to give Rose her last wish, that we would find our way back to each other one day. That this wasn't the end.

I should have said a lot more than what I did, but in that moment I was truly speechless, a part of me felt that it was always too good to be true, then I felt so selfish for even thinking that. So selfish for being concerned about how we would get through this, when she was about to lose the most important person in her life.

We laid together in each other's arms for what felt like a lifetime, neither of us said anything. Eventually Alex started to pack her things, she was going to stay with her grandma for the next few days whilst they got everything sorted out.

Who would run the bar? What would she do about her grandma's house? Where would they stay in Cannon Beach? There was so many things not finalised, but this was something that could not wait.

The next day, saying goodbye was the hardest, the girl I had really fallen for was moving half way across the country. Okay, so it wasn't quite half way across the country, but Oregon was five hours away by plane, that to me felt like the other side of the world.

I was about to start my career in Raleigh, and architecture wasn't a simple 9-5 job with weekends free. I would be doing long hours to begin with, trying to prove myself and show everyone what I could do. I'd have no time to travel that far, but it was only three months I told myself. I hoped for Alex's sake that it was longer because with all my heart I wished that Rose would stay in this world for as long as possible.

We spoke the night before about whether we should continue the relationship as long distance, or whether we should call a time out whilst this was all happening, but neither of us could bring ourselves to take a break. We knew what we had was something special, the thought of not having her in my life, not texting her or talking to her it broke my heart. We would make long distance work, we had too. The other choice was just not acceptable.

"I'm going to miss you so much Kacy, you have no idea. I'll talk to you and text you every day, don't worry we can get through this."

She hugged me and I didn't want to let go, I embraced every part of her, a sudden rush of emotions came over me. I couldn't let her leave without telling her how I really felt.

"Alex….."   "Kaci…."

We spoke each other's name in unison, eager to tell the

other what we were both feeling deep inside. The look in both our eyes gave it away there was no need for the words that would follow.

"I have fallen in love with you Alex, I know it's only been a short time. I know that there is so much that needs to be worked out, but I want to be with you no matter what."

I looked into her beautiful face and I saw a sudden realisation that she too was in love with me.

"I am so in love with you too, meeting you that night was the best night of my life. You have shown me what it feels like to want someone else's happiness over my own. To want to be with someone every second of every day. I know we are just beginning, but there is so much more for us."

She was so sincere and heartfelt whenever she spoke like that, I often thought she could write a pretty decent love story, maybe our love story, one day. I couldn't contain the smile upon my face, this perfect girl felt exactly the same way that I did.

"I will miss you so much." I told myself to not get upset, this was just the start and when she eventually came back to Raleigh, however heartbroken she may be, we could work through it together. I would be there for her, I promised her that.

"I'll miss you too, more than ever. I'll call you later tonight. I think we are going to set off first thing in the morning and stay at a B&B for a few nights, until the beach house is ready."

She pulled me in close to her, our body's fit perfectly into one another like two separate pieces of a puzzle, coming together again. The way she cradled my face and lifted it up towards her lips to kiss them so tenderly was pure bliss. I always did like that I was a few inches smaller than her, Alex had always made me feel so safe and protected from anything bad that could happen.

I was indestructible when I was in her arms. We spent a minute like that, savouring every last taste of her lips on mine until my heaven was broken and it was time for her to leave.

I waved her goodbye as she drove off into the sun, wondering when I would see her again, hoping that it would be soon.

I had truly fallen in love with Alex Dawson, I had fallen in love with her heart, her soul and her body. The courage she possessed, the confidence that shone through her and the overwhelming kindness that was evident to anyone that knew her. Just a few quality's taken from a long, ever-growing list that made her who she was.

In that moment when my world felt upside down, when my head couldn't make sense of what would become, I told myself that I would always be in love with her, even if she turned out to be something else, even if the world painted a picture of her that should not be. I would still love her, I knew this then and I would know it always.

CHAPTER FOUR

Kacy,

I miss you even more today than I did yesterday, I wish this was easier. My grandma is still doing great, she has surpassed the two month mark today and the doctors said she could live for at very least another two months, she's a wonder is our Rose. Every day I get to wake up and see her smile and it's the greatest feeling in the world knowing she is somewhere she loves, a place full of memories and she's continuing to make them with her family around her. It warms my heart so much.

Thank you for checking in on the bar for me, I ring

them almost every day, but I worry they are just lying to me to keep me quiet. I was talking about you yesterday, all good things of course.

I can't believe it's been 2 months since I saw your beautiful face. I want so much to book a flight to North Carolina tomorrow just so I can see you and kiss you, but I can't risk not being here if something was to happen, I would never forgive myself. I hope you understand.

Take some time off work? Come and see me for a few days? I wish so much that you could! The plan you sent in your last letter looks amazing, I can see you have really worked hard on it, I don't know much about architecture, but I'd hire you in an instant.

Next week me and Natalie are taking Rose into town, there is a carnival on which should be fun. I think she's really excited because she remembers going there with Grandpa over 20 years ago now. It will be nice to take her out, she's restricted as to what she can do lately we don't want to make her feel any worse or open her up to any sort of virus, that could make things complicated, but she insists on going. I don't think she wants to be stuck up in the house all day, every day and I don't blame her. I plan on meeting a friend too, her name is Jennifer Locksley, someone me and Nat grew up with down here. Whenever we came for the summer her family would be here too, so that will be nice to catch up. This is only a short and sweet letter, I will be ringing you tonight anyway because I can't physically go a day without hearing that voice.

I hope you know that no matter what I am always here for you, I may be far away, but I am with you in your heart and I intend to stay there for a very long time. You are the first thing I think about when I wake up and the last thing before I go to sleep at night. You truly are my dream, my reality and my future. Whatever you do today, tomorrow and every day for the rest of your life just always know one thing, I will always love you.

Yours always,
A x

I always did love waking up to find a letter from Alex. Two whole months she had been gone and not once did it get any easier. I missed her terribly every single day. It was after the first few weeks that we decided to start writing to one another, we both liked the idea of having letters to read, especially when we felt lost or alone.

We liked the thought of not just talking on the phone when sometimes words can be lost, but writing them down as well, so we could go back to them year after year and remember the time we spent apart.

We wrote at least twice a week, Alex more than me, she didn't have a lot to do on the coast. Most of the time she would just sit with her grandma, they would read or play cards, maybe even watch some television. Grandma Rose would usually go to bed around 8 pm, at this time Alex would write to me. It filled me with such a sense of happiness and excitement when I read her letters.

We spoke most days on the phone so things written may have already been told, but that didn't matter to me. I loved everything she wrote. I liked to imagine her sat up in bed or sat by the window watching the world go by, as her pen so elegantly graced the pieces of paper.

We talked about seeing each other on several occasions, but it was just too difficult at the time. I was a new intern and holidays were not permitted for the first six months and a weekend was simply not enough time to visit either. I worked it out that by the time I arrived in Oregon, it would be almost time to fly back home, for work the next day.

My work was my priority with Alex gone. I worked twelve hour shifts most days, I didn't want to sit at home and miss her. I needed to occupy my mind. I figured the best way to do that was to throw myself into my work. It paid off for me I must admit. Within the first few months I was noticed by several members of the hierarchy. It was after all going to be my career, so making a great impression was of the upmost importance.

The good news was that Rose was doing better than expected by the doctors. Originally she was given 2-3 months, she had already gotten past two months much to the delight of her grandchildren. On her latest check-up she was exceeding expectations. The doctors then predicted she could continue until the same time next year, providing she kept healthy and didn't partake in any strenuous activities. I was so relieved for Alex, I know how happy it was making her spending every day with her grandma. I can't imagine what it must be like to lose a parent or a grandparent. I luckily enough hadn't had to go through that traumatic experience, but I imagine that just like Alex, I would be grateful for every single day and every last smile I got to witness with that person.

I wasn't religious, but lately I had been praying that when the day came, Alex would find peace in the late memories she had with Rose.

I was so thankful that nothing had changed between us, you never know how a relationship is going to cope when it becomes long distance. There was a thousand different endings to ponder when I thought about me and Alex, as our story started to unravel what would we become? The best part was knowing that the story was not a story, about me or about her, but about us. A story about how much Alex had become a part of my life, the memories we had created already and the ever growing feelings we felt for one another, which I knew would echo in eternity, never fading and never changing. Just like my love for her.

My heart sank the moment I realised just how much I wanted her, how much I needed her. She moved me in a way that was breath-taking to me, in a way that made every other woman on this planet seem so pale and incomparable beside her.

I started to write a journal the day that Alex left, I hadn't written one since I was about seventeen years old, but a part of me felt the need to put my words and my feelings in a place that was private. I felt relief when I wrote in my journal, like I was getting something off my chest in order to clear my mind. I seemed to make more sense of things that way.

Besides what else did I have to do? The answer to that question would be, not a great deal.

I would often find myself sat in bed at night, so wide awake, my brain was doing overtime and the only way around that was to write. Maybe once a week I would watch a film with Whitney or with my mum, I did go out one night for Whitney's birthday, but other than that I was always so exhausted. I worked ridiculously long hours and the only person that could really tempt me to interact after a thirteen hour shift would be Alex. Some days we simply didn't speak at all, they were the worst days to get through.

By the time I finished work she would already be asleep. Alex slowly fell into the same routine as her grandma, who would get up at 5 am every morning and be in bed by 9 pm. I always found it difficult when I couldn't speak to her. Those days almost felt wasted.

Later that same day I gave Alex a call, it was always when I finished work usually around 7 pm, so I expected her to be back at home. It took her a while to answer, but when she did it was so great to hear her voice.

"Alex, I've missed your voice so much."

"Kacy, my beautiful girl, I've missed yours too." I could tell the excitement in her voice, was just as genuine as my own. That made me smile.

"How was your day at the carnival?"

There was a slight pause on the line before she answered, the signal was not great in areas. I could hear a faint sound of music and laughing in the background, it made it rather hard for me to hear her every word.

"Babe it's been great, Rose had so much fun, watching the parade was her favourite part. I don't think I've ever seen her laugh so much, it completely warmed my heart. She ended up telling me so many stories about her and Grandpa, she told me about the moment they first met, the moment she knew she loved him, I could see her reliving it all, it was so sweet. I will tell you about it all someday." I could hear in her voice how happy that made her, which in turn made me happy. All she asked for towards the end was that her Grandma enjoyed every last day, I knew Alex would do everything in her power to ensure that.

"That's great Al, I'm so happy for you and I can't wait to hear the stories, write them in your next letter. I'm sure it would make great reading…..can you hear me?.....What is all that racket in the background? I can hardly hear you talk."

"Sorry babe I didn't realise it was so loud, I'm back in town at the carnival there's an after party, my grandma insisted I come back once I took her home, she claims she wants to see me have some fun and at 23 I shouldn't be going to bed every night at the same time as her. Although believe it or not it's been rather refreshing I feel like I'm 16 again." She laughed to herself, to be fair Rose did have a point, I know she must have been very persuasive to get Alex to leave her side for the evening. "Aww that's nice Al, it sounds fun there, I wish I was with you! Is Natalie there too?"

I tried to sound upbeat at the idea of her out having fun without me, I know she deserved it, but I couldn't help the twinge of jealousy in my stomach, knowing I wasn't there by her side. I couldn't bring myself to go out and have fun without her. It just wasn't the same anymore, I would find myself constantly thinking about her, just wishing I was home so I could talk to her on the phone.

She quickly replied with no delay from the signal this time.

"No babe, Natalie is at home with Rose I told her to ring me if she needed anything at all, but she insisted I come. The old friend I told you about, Jennifer? Well she's here too and a group of her friends, so I have some company. I really wish you were here too!"

I could hear people shouting her in the background, was that Jennifer? I couldn't help but feel a sudden rush of jealousy, before I could even dig a little deeper there was a quick and muffled goodbye before the signal was lost. I tried to call back, but no answer, so I sent a goodnight text before my head hit the pillow. I was so tired I couldn't bear to think or stress over what Alex was doing, or if she was still missing me. I had often given good advice to friends when it came to relationships, I think at that point it was time to take some of the best advice I could give, something I truly believed.

Whatever will be, will be.

Simple words to some, but a meaning so deep and true to the core.

Several days went by before we next spoke, our schedules had been so conflicting we found it hard to talk on the phone, we sent the odd text throughout the day just to check in, but the longer we went without talking the less real our relationship felt. A part of me started to question what she was doing, and who she was with, did she still feel the same way I did?

The things that will go through someone's mind at the first sign of insecurity or doubt is remarkable. I really did love this girl, but I asked myself at the time what if things were to stay this way for another six months or even a year. Would we make it through that? What about when she came back after all that time with a heavy heart at the loss of her beloved grandma, would she still be the same person? From the bottom of my heart a month ago I would have said yes, without a doubt, but now as the days rolled on and our contact became less frequent, I almost felt like she was slipping away.

I received a letter from her exactly a week after the last one, a letter that filled me with love and joy. A letter that made all the doubts I had fade away, for the 5 minutes it took to read over every word. It went like this;

Kacy,

If you know nothing else in this world, just know that I love you with every ounce of my being. I hope that you realize your importance to me and to everyone who has ever had the privilege of knowing you. I hope you know that whenever you are feeling down I am here for you and that I only ever strive to make you happy. You bring out the best parts of me and you make me believe that dreams really do come true.

Being with you gives me a reason to believe in all the wonderful things this world has to offer, I only see it now because of the light you bring to my life, because of the pure happiness you make me feel. I intend on staying in your life for as long as you will have me. If that is forever then forever I will stay and that will never change. I'll leave you with one thing I want you to always remember. Whatever you do today or any day, never forget one thing, I will <u>always</u> love you.

I promise,
A x

Just like that, any doubts I had were gone. It only took those perfect words to reassure me that she still felt the same way. She still wanted all the same things we had always wanted. That was until I saw the date in the corner, 10/09/2010. The letter must have gotten lost in the post, the date that day was 29/09/2010, a full nineteen days after she had wrote that letter. Nineteen days ago everything was great, but lately I didn't know what to make of it. The letter all of a sudden was not a realisation that everything I had been worrying about was non-existent, but a realisation that nothing had changed, and so the gut feelings of paranoia and doubt came flooding back. I hated that feeling.

I called Alex later that day on my dinner break, I wanted to tell her that I missed her, that I loved her, I just wanted everything to go back to normal, I wanted to believe that it was all in my head and that nothing had changed between us. I had a speech planned that quickly disappeared, when the phone rang straight through to voicemail.

Why wasn't her phone on? Was her battery dead? I had no other way of contacting her other than her mobile phone, I didn't have her sister's number so I couldn't contact her either. A part of me really started to worry, Alex wouldn't have ever let her phone die, she always wanted to talk to me or text me at every opportunity she got, sometimes when I finished work I would have five or six messages. The past two days I had received just one lousy text message. A text that simply read;

From: My Alex

Today has been a good day, I've met some nice people here. My grandma is the happiest I've ever seen her since grandpa died. Later today I'm taking her into town again to see a theatre show.
Jennifer works at the local theatre so she gets free tickets, Rose is so excited. I hope your days going well. Speak soon babe.
I miss you. A x

Then I had gotten nothing back after that. I didn't like how she kept mentioning Jennifer's name, it seemed she was spending the majority of her free time with her lately. Was that the reason she was being distant? Had she found someone else to occupy her time? I hated myself for thinking like that, I had never been the jealous type before, but with Alex I couldn't help it. I was so worried that Jennifer was moving her way in on my girlfriend. I didn't have any evidence though, nor any reason to question Alex about it. I quickly put the thoughts to the back of my mind, I didn't know Jennifer, she could be a lovely person, and she could have a boyfriend/girlfriend or be married or even have children. I didn't really know anything about her, so who was I to judge what I didn't know. I refused to let myself feel this way, not without any concrete evidence to support it. The fact that my head was all over the place, just made things a lot worse when they didn't need to be.

I needed to get in touch with Alex, I needed her reassurance. I needed her to tell me that she loved me and that everything would be okay.

I went on with my day at work, pushing everything to the back of my mind as best I could. I had to concentrate on the new block of apartments I was designing. After the success of my first building design, my boss felt it necessary to give me more of a challenge, something he had never done before with an intern, especially not an intern who had only been at the company a mere two months.

I had been trusted with designing a very upscale, high class block of apartments, standing eight floors tall with two penthouse suites at the very top and a middle floor that contained a bar, restaurant, gym and a swimming pool. The description of what the company wanted was extravagant, for one apartment you were talking a price tag in the region of $400,000. My dad had designed something similar a few years back, so I always had him for any support or advice about what the company would want to see.

I finished work around 7 pm and still I had no reply from Alex, no missed call, not even a text to say sorry I missed your call. I know that signal wasn't great where she was, so I occasionally let her off for the late replies and constant talks with her voicemail, but this was getting slightly ridiculous now.

I tried her again, this time her phone didn't go straight to voicemail, an unfamiliar voice answered after the first few rings.

"Hello, can I help you?"

"Hi, is Alex there please?" Who was this woman answering Alex's phone?

"No sorry, this is Jennifer. Alex isn't here, she left her phone at my house last night. I can get her to give you a call back if you like?"

Jennifer? Why was Alex at Jennifer's last night? Is that why she didn't speak to me? My heart sank into my stomach at the realisation that maybe I was right.

"It's okay, erm...could you just tell her that Kacy tried calling please."

"Of course no problem Kacy, you have a great day now, goodbye." She sounded like some automated service,

~ 66 ~

the fakeness in her tone of voice worried me. Was this really happening? I told myself not to jump to conclusions, not until I had the chance to speak to Alex, maybe she could clear all this up and put it down to a huge misunderstanding.

Did I think I was being a little optimistic? Yes I did, I always felt that you should believe your gut over your head or even your heart for that matter. Your head will always make excuses, it will always justify what the other person has done. The heart will also make excuses, simply because it loves that person and more than likely you have given it to that person. The gut however, is the truest of all, it will not lie, it will not make excuses, the gut feeling you get is the one you should trust, I believe it's almost always correct.

I lay awake until 10 pm that night, still I had no response from Alex. There was only so much television I could watch to distract my mind, it was time to go to sleep. I wouldn't wait up any longer nor would I put myself through this anymore. I was a strong person and Alex had one more chance, if she didn't contact me the next day and explain everything to me then I was done. I refused to let her know that this hurt me, I wouldn't give someone the satisfaction of knowing how upset I was, of knowing how much it was truly effecting me. If she didn't care enough then neither would I. It may be easier said than done, but I knew I could do it, besides life moves on swiftly and that would be with or without

Alex. After four missed calls and six text messages, the choice was now hers.

CHAPTER FIVE

Journal entry:

I had never felt this way before, no one had ever made my heart ache and my head hurt. I couldn't understand it anymore, why was she being so different with me? Why all of a sudden was there no contact from her? If Jennifer had something to do with this, if she had fallen in love with someone else, why wouldn't she just tell me? Maybe she didn't want to face it? I know many people might handle a situation that way, but not Alex, I thought she was so different. I didn't think she could ever hurt me, I should of known that everything was too perfect to be true, that she was to perfect. There was nothing else for me to do now, she had always been inevitable to me and no matter how hard I tried to stay away, everything always came back to her. She was the love of my life, the reason for my existence, at least I thought she was.

I guess things change.

All my journal entries over the past three months had been happy. In fact they were more than happy, they were entries about love, art and passion. Everything that had been re-awakened in my heart since I met Alex. That was no longer possible, I couldn't bring myself to write any words of inspiration or anything that would remotely help me move forward. I had deleted Alex from my phonebook, I decided to take the upgrade that had been due for the past four months so I now had a new number, which I sent to everyone in my phonebook bar Alex.

Maybe I was being too hasty, trust me it wasn't the easiest thing I'd ever done, to cut someone out of your life piece by piece, especially someone that you truly loved, it's probably the hardest thing I've ever had to do. My friends agreed that nothing seemed to add up, I had explained everything down to the minor details and they couldn't understand where things had gone wrong.

They told me I shouldn't give up, that I should fly out there and get some answers, but I wasn't willing to put myself through that embarrassment. I prided myself on three things, being strong, courageous and confident. I always had. They were three words that anyone who knew me well enough would use to describe me. I thought that I would never be anything but those things, I guess that was easier said than done. Even If I myself knew at that moment in time I may not be those things, when it came to Alex, I certainly wouldn't have anyone else think that.

If ever Alex were to come back, I wouldn't let her know of the way my heart had broken into a million pieces. She wouldn't have the satisfaction of knowing how I stayed up crying at night, struggling to sleep because my mind wouldn't stop overthinking anything and everything to do with her. I had no other choice but to move on with my life, it had been almost two weeks since I last had contact with her. I had no idea if she had tried to contact me because my number was no longer the same, but I had not received any letters from her so my suspicions must have been correct. She had just forgotten about me, she had simply moved on and found someone new without so much as a goodbye or even I'm sorry, to ease the blow.

That to me was the only explanation. I wouldn't let it ruin me, I had too much going for me to spend the rest of my life pining for someone that wouldn't do the same for me. From that point onwards, I vowed a new me.

My mum knew how down I had been the past few weeks, so she decided to surprise me with a spa day to Synergy Spa, it was just what I needed. We both booked on for the Full Monty treatment that included skin-care, nail-care, massage, manicure and pedicure. When you add in lunch and champagne prepared for in between treatments, it was a glorious day out. It was so relaxing to be able to sit with a glass of champagne and do nothing, but be pampered all day long. It didn't quite take away the pain, but what better way to get back at someone who's hurt you than looking the best you possibly could?

My mum had always been my best friend too, there was nothing I didn't tell her. A part of her really disliked Alex for what she had done, at first I didn't like the way she spoke about the girl I loved, but I slowly came to realise that she was the one person in this whole world that had my best interests at heart.

I met up with Whitney that same week. I had gone into hibernation after cutting Alex from my life. It was my way of dealing with the situation, but now it was time to come back out and there was no better way to do that, than a Starbucks, and mall trip with my best friend.

I met Whitney at Starbucks around midday, her face lit up with an amazing pearly white smile when she saw me coming.

"Seriously girl, it's so good to see you. You have been hiding away for too long."

"I know Whit, I'm so sorry I've been distant lately, it's

just been difficult."

I smiled my best I'm okay now smile hoping she wouldn't hound me for too many details. There was not one day were Whitney didn't bombard me with text messages, we were so used to seeing each other daily. This new chapter in my life didn't allow for that not just because of my job, but because of the horrible feeling I got every time I thought about entertaining someone, other than the snuggly brown teddy bear I'd had since I was 8.

"I know hunny, but don't push me away though okay? You're my best friend, I'm here for you no matter what, any hour of the day, 7 days a week and don't you ever forget that. Even if you want me to sit by your side whilst you cry, or bring you ice cream and watch you throw up after you eat the whole tub in one go. That's what I'm here for."

She truly meant it too, Whitney was by far the best friend anyone could ever hope for, the fact she was so understanding and perfect about it all, made me feel guilty for pushing her away.

"I won't again, I promise. Bringing me ice cream sounds nice. I used to like being ill when we were younger, I knew you'd turn up with my favourite Ben & Jerry's cookie dough." I smiled at the many memories we had together.

"Good, well I can always bring you ice cream you just say the word and I'm there.....So have you heard from Alex at all?" she said with a sympathetic glare. A quick change of subject I would rather not discuss, but I knew she meant well.

"No, the only way she could contact me now would be through a letter and she hasn't done that, so I guess I was right all along Whit."

"I'm so sorry Kacy, I think you have a lot more self-respect than I do. I wouldn't stop until I got to the bottom of what's happened. I'd want that Jennifer bitch to pay."

That was Whitney for you, she was certainly very hot-headed. I on the other hand was not, I thought it better to take myself out of the situation, in my eyes it was her loss and that's all I continued to tell myself.

"What's done is done Whit, I guess you never really know someone as well as you think you do. Who needs her anyway when I've got amazing friends like you? Don't forget the pact, if I get to 30 and I'm still single, me and you are getting married. I don't care if you're married with kids by then, we will have an affair."

We both stuck our little fingers out, solemnly swearing our pinky promise. It was a running joke that Whitney would become a lesbian at 30, on the off chance that we were both still single, we would just marry each other. We figured it sounded like a good idea after seeing it on the TV programme Friends one evening. I tried as best I could to seem like I was getting over it when I myself knew I definitely wasn't.

"That's right hunny Mrs & Mrs Sullivan, has a nice ring to it I think....hey do you know what amazing friends like me do? We take our best friends out on the town to help them recover from broken hearts. There is no better way to get over someone than getting under someone else. Now I come to think of it, I can't have you being single at 30, I don't think I'd swing that way even for a hot piece of ass like yourself." Whitney gave me a cheeky wink, she was always so bubbly and positive she really made me feel so much better about everything. Trust me when I say at that time I didn't fancy "getting under someone else" but I really did appreciate her efforts. A night out with Whitney was always a good one, half of the time you might wake up somewhere unusual or barely remember anything that happened, but I guess that was the sign of an eventful evening.

"What do you have in mind?"

"I'm thinking this Friday, we go to Icon, pre-drinks at your place of course. I will do all the inviting and I'll pick up the drinks, plus we are in the mall right now so we can shop for a new outfit. Nothing too over the top though, if I remember right Icon is very casual on a Friday night isn't it?"

"Yeah Whit, I already have some clothes I bought last month that I haven't worn. A night out sounds great, I think it's just what I need." The more I thought about it the more I was beginning to look forward to it. Pre-drinks were always at my house because I had a huge second lounge/dining area with a bar, so it was always the place to go before a night out. I didn't mind at all and neither did my parents, they liked the house being lively every now and again.

I knew Whitney would take care of everything, she had decided lately she wanted to be a party planner. I backed her 100% she was after all fantastic at planning a birthday or a night out. It was quite a huge step from a Lawyer or a Model, but Whitney was always great at achieving whatever she put her mind to. I could definitely picture her being the latest celebrity party planner, rubbing shoulders with the likes of Beyoncé and Jay Z, I would definitely need an invite to those parties. Friday soon came around, when you work twelve hour days you soon wonder where your week has gone. I did think to myself maybe I should cut down on work, I was only twenty one years old after all, I should have been enjoying my life, going out with friends and making memories, but work was my distraction. It was my only way of not thinking about Alex and I couldn't say that it wasn't paying off, because it was. I had been noticed countless times by people higher up hence why I had been given the new apartment complex, there was an upside to every downside.

I had already picked out my outfit, skinny jeans, a tee, and my leather jacket. I didn't fancy wearing a dress that night, I know some of the other girls would be, but I was more than comfortable going casual.

I received a text from Whitney with the details of the evening, everyone would be at mine around 8 pm and a taxi was already booked for 10 pm to take us all into town. I had a list of the girls coming over to my house beforehand these were; Brooke, Chloe, Jessica, Lauren and Lara. The last one I had to double check with Whitney and I found it was in fact my ex-girlfriend Lara. She had recently become close friends with Jessica and you would rarely see them without each other on a night out. I didn't have a problem with her coming over or spending the evening in her company, what went on between us was almost a lifetime ago, there was certainly no hard feelings. Speak of the devil, I received a text from her almost five minutes after getting off the phone with Whitney.

From: Lara C

Hey Stranger. I'm looking forward to a good night out tonight, I hope it's okay that I come over to yours with everyone else. I feel like I haven't seen you in forever it will be nice to catch up. Let me know if you need me to bring anything over. Although I think Whitney has the drinks covered ha-ha
See you later.

Lara x

Lara was so sweet, I had to give her that. I don't know why we didn't speak much after we broke up, it was a mutual thing that we were both okay about. I guess we both just figured that nothing good really came from ex's being friends, but a part of me was excited to see her again that night, besides she was really good-looking, funny and kind. It made me wonder for a moment why it never actually worked out with her.
I quickly replied to her message before I started to get ready. Brooke was the first to arrive, early as always, I

swear she spent the whole day getting ready, because she was never late, or even on time for that matter. She was always at least an hour before anyone else. Shortly after 8 pm everyone had arrived, there was a sort of buzz and an atmosphere in the room, the evening was going to be a crazy one. I sensed it from the get go. I started to put all the drinks in the fridge and get the ice bucket ready. Whitney had brought an array of drinks including champagne, rose wine, Jack Daniels, vodka and a number of mixers. Clearly she planned on not remembering any part of the evening.

Lara approached me after five minutes, I had to hand it to her, she looked great. Lara had a style very similar to Alex from the neck down she could even be mistaken for Alex. I'm not sure how that made me feel, I still got the familiar twinge in my stomach when I thought about Alex or even worse when something reminded me of her. I wasn't sure if that would ever go away, in time I imagined it would.

"Hey Kacy, how have you been?"

"Hello you, I'm okay thank you, have you been up to much these days?"

"Not a great deal, working most of the time to be honest totally living the dream." She said that last bit sarcastically, which made me laugh.

"Where do you work now?"

"I'm working at Ralph Lauren, they offered me the Managers Job and well I get discount off the clothing so I could hardly say no could I." She gestured towards the outfit she was wearing which was in fact 90% Ralph Lauren product.

"Oh well I know where to come now then don't I." I gave Lara a cheeky wink to show I was joking, well half joking, it certainly could benefit having a friend who gets discount at Ralph Lauren.

"Anytime K, it'd be nice to spend some time with you, we could maybe grab some lunch or something next time you're heading into town? I'm really glad you're coming along tonight." Lara wasn't the type to beat around the bush, if she wanted something she would go straight for it. I knew this because at one time I was that something she wanted. Although to anyone listening, grabbing lunch sounded innocent, the look in Lara's eyes and the way she touched my hand as I poured us a drink said otherwise. I almost responded unthinkably with a no until I quickly realised I had no reason to say no anymore, I had no ties, I was single and free to do as I pleased.

"Me too I need to let my hair down a little, I've been told more than once. Lunch sounds nice, I'd like that, shall I just text you when I'm free?"

"Yeah let's do that. So you're looking forward to tonight then?"

I handed Lara a drink consisting of Vodka and Lemonade, I remembered from when we used to date that it was her favourite. It's funny the things you remember about someone even if you haven't been in contact with them for a long, long time. She glanced towards the drink, curiosity in her smile.

"You think I don't remember your favourite drink? Or has it changed? I mean it has been a while."

I hoped that it was still the same so I didn't look stupid when I was trying to be cool and carefree. Luckily for me it was, I continued to talk to Lara until the taxi arrived I received more than one look from my friends, topped off by Whitney's comment as we walked toward the Taxi.

"Looks like inviting Lara was my best idea yet." She nudged my arm and lifted her head back in silent laughter. She certainly found it amusing and from what I can remember she did just about everything in her power, to make the night more about me and Lara than anything else, that was Whitney. I honestly wouldn't have expected anything less.

The night turned out to be so much fun, half the population of Raleigh seemed to be out, so many people I hadn't seen since high school or college. I even bumped into an old friend who used to live across from me, it was at least seven years since I last saw her. I spent most of the evening talking to familiar faces, sharing old memories with one another amongst a sea of drinks. Before I knew it the evening was coming to a close, I was so glad I had been persuaded to go out, it seemed Icon was the place to be that night and it made me realise even more so that life does move on. There are plenty of other people waiting around the corner, more opportunity's waiting to be discovered because life is never over until your eyes close forever, anything other than that is simply a temporary mishap that in time will fix itself.

There was a quote printed on the back of my bedroom door that had always stuck with me, it simply read.

"I believe that everything happens for a reason. People change so that you can learn to let go, things go wrong so that you appreciate them when they're right, you believe lies so you eventually learn to trust no one but yourself and sometimes good things fall apart so better things can fall together."

Marilyn Monroe

Marilyn certainly hit the nail on the head with that one. No quote had ever touched me like that. There was something in it that anyone, anywhere could relate to. The last part "sometimes good things fall apart so better things can fall together" was the bit that really hit home. Thinking that something better would fall together was the only thing keeping me from breaking down. I hoped that people all over the world suffering from broken hearts or struggling with any kind of difficulty would read that quote and know that it will get better, that you have to think positive and believe that everything does happen for a reason, the reason may be unknown at first but in time it will reveal itself.

I took a taxi back to my house at around 3 pm with

Whitney, Jessica and Lara in tow. Rather than have them get a taxi all the way back home I said they could stay at mine. It wasn't a problem, I had spare bedrooms and I had a king-size bed to which Whitney usually jumped straight in. My parents didn't mind people staying over as long as we didn't wake up the whole house when we got home. Besides my brother usually liked the amount of half-naked woman, walking around the house the next morning, so I reassured everyone it wasn't a big deal.

Funnily enough one by one everybody went to sleep, until it was just me and Lara left. Whitney had done her usual raising of the eyebrows, before she trotted off to get comfortable in my bed. This basically meant 'don't do anything I wouldn't do, but if you do make sure you tell me all about it in the morning' I had figured out all the many faces of my best friend over the years. I think we barely communicated with words anymore, one quick look could mean so much more than a paragraph of words.

I had shown her to the guest bedroom where she would stay earlier on and although I could see she was tired, she certainly didn't show any signs of retreating to bed for the night. We stayed up a little longer talking about a variety of things, the sore subject of Alex was spoken about for a few minutes until I deliberately changed the subject. Anyone in their right mind would be curious as to what had happened between us, I rarely mentioned anything, I often went quiet if the subject did ever crop up. I guess it was just my own way of dealing with the situation. I found it easier to push it to the back of my mind and keep it there for as long as I possibly could. I told people that long distance hadn't worked out and I wouldn't speak any further on the topic, nobody had to know the ins and outs. I imagine it would only cause that dreaded awkward silence and I couldn't speak for anyone else but I certainly didn't want that.

Whitney was the only person who knew the whole truth, well as much of the truth as I myself actually knew, after all there was no concrete evidence as to why or who had made us split up, or even if we had split up, there had been no official breaking up. It almost felt like an unresolved problem, which in turn just made it even more difficult to move forward. How could I possibly gain any closure from this situation? That was a question I was not sure I would be able to answer. I'd try my damned hardest I knew that for sure. Starting that night, it might not be what people class as closure, but it certainly helped me move forward.

The night did not end at 4 am when I finally declared I was going to bed. It ended at 6 am with me in the guest room accompanied by Lara, it was certainly a morning to remember. Although my body was still filled with an incredible amount of alcohol, both of our body's for that matter, that didn't contribute in the slightest. If I knew one thing it was how familiar Lara was to me, I had already had a sexual relationship with her so nothing was unusual, nothing was awkward it was just two people enjoying each other's company. I wouldn't class it as a one night stand or a mistake, it was an inevitable happening, a simple act of passion that was too overwhelming for two human beings to deny.

I lay there in her arms afterwards, enjoying the comfort of somebody else. I hadn't felt this way in what seemed like a decade.

"Are you okay? I wasn't really expecting that to happen."

"Are you complaining?" I teased.

"Definitely not, it kind of makes me realise what I've been missing." She gave me the sexiest smirk I'd ever laid eyes on, I could tell she had enjoyed the night just as much as I had. After that I lay there rather quiet, the guilt I felt was overwhelming. A noticeable tear rolled down my left cheek landing on Alex's stomach beneath me.

"What's wrong? Do you want me to leave? You've been so quiet I thought you were sleeping for a minute."

"I'm just overwhelmed I guess, a part of me feels guilty, which sounds stupid because I haven't done anything wrong, she was the one who did something wrong." I realised I had said too much, I didn't want to talk about my relationship with Alex especially not with the woman I had just slept with. I wiped the tears from my eyes and looked up into Lara's.

"I don't want you to leave, this is the most comfortable I've felt in a long time, thank you for being here with me." she too wiped the last remaining tear from my cheek bone and smiled.

"Then I'll stay for as long as you need me too. I won't pry, but you can talk to me if you wish okay?"

"Thanks Lara." I gave her a quick kiss and retreated back to her stomach, where I quickly fell asleep. I appreciated the fact she didn't question anything. She wasn't trying to get the latest gossip like most people would. A part of me hoped that she saw the whole thing the same way that I did, I didn't want to hurt anyone's feelings or lead anybody on, I wasn't that type of girl. What I needed right then was comfort and familiarity, but with no strings attached maybe I was asking for too much, or maybe I had found the perfect person who would want the exact same things as me. Right then I could only hope.

CHAPTER SIX

My life really was beginning to move forward. There was definitely some improvement at the very least. My friends and family had helped in more ways than one, always keeping me occupied when I wasn't at work, it got to the point were I hardly ever thought about Alex. I think there would always be the heartache in the pit of my stomach when I thought of her, maybe that would always be there or maybe with a little more time I would forget all together. Right then I could've only hoped for the latter.

It had been two months to the day since I'd had any contact with her. Which only proved to me just how much the relationship meant and how special it had been, because despite the constant distractions a part of me still wished to see her again. I guess I hadn't had closure after all.

Lara had helped me move on, she knew the fragile state I was in, she knew that I wasn't looking for a relationship or anything remotely complicated. I wanted simplicity for once in my life, no drama, no arguments just an easy mutual agreement. Luckily for me that was exactly what Lara had wanted too, we spoke about what had happened several weeks ago at my house, we both laid all the cards out on the table and decided we would continue to see each other, but we wouldn't make it a big deal. We wouldn't make it into something that it wasn't.

I know what everybody was thinking, that could never work. Surprisingly enough for me and Lara it did, we saw each other several times a week, she usually came over to mine or we would go to the cinema or for something to eat. It was nice and just what I needed. My friends started to grow suspicious after the first week, constant questions about what was happening with us. When I simply told them "We are just having fun, nothing more to it than that." I received a chorus of odd looks and "You know that will never work Kacy." Almost every single time.

The one person who actually agreed with me was of course my best friend, Whitney had in a roundabout way told me I had needs and I had to do what makes me happy, and to not bog myself down worrying about the final outcome. I guess she was right in a way, if we all worried too much about how something would end or how it may go wrong, then we'd never do it and that would be a tragedy in itself. To miss out on life because we were too scared to hurt or be hurt was not an option.

I was always thankful to have her, she really was one of the most amazing people I had ever known.

I went downstairs that morning after finishing my usual routine. After a good few months my morning work routine was now down to an amazing one hour, which for me was a complete and utter miracle. My hair alone on a good day could take 45 minutes to get it perfectly wavy, I had started tying it up on a morning now, it was so much easier and a lot less time consuming. I would always spend ten minutes around the breakfast bar with my mum whilst I ate my breakfast, that morning she had made me two chocolate filled croissants, they were always the best way to start the day. I may have been nearly twenty two years old, but my mum still made me breakfast every morning, did all my washing, ironed my clothes and made me lunch to take to work. These were just a few perks of living at home. She liked to be needed and I certainly needed her, so in my eyes it worked out perfectly for both of us.

My mum looked different that morning, her usually smiley exterior was slightly less bubbly, I could tell she had something on her mind. She had even refrained from dressing like a red-carpet superstar which was incredibly unusual to say the least. As I started to eat my second croissant she revealed what that was.

"Kacy sweetie, I have a few letters for you, please don't get upset with me, I have seen lately how well you've been getting on and I didn't want you to get upset again, but I think that Alex has sent you some letters."

From the look on my mother's face she didn't think, she knew that Alex had sent them otherwise she wouldn't have kept it a secret.

"What? When? Why didn't you tell me mum?"

I was in shock I thought that for the past two months Alex hadn't attempted to contact me that she had just moved on like we were nothing, as if I had meant nothing. My mother began to explain;

"The first one came a week after it all happened, it was actually a genuine mistake by your father, it got mixed up in some of his post and you know what he's like it gets put in his office and left there, he only came across it on his desk about 3 weeks later. By that time I didn't want to mention it to you, I didn't know what would be for the best. Then another letter came about a month after the first and then another a week after that but nothing since then. I'm so sorry I didn't tell you sooner sweetheart, I wanted to protect you. I thought that reading the letters would bring everything back up and you seemed to be moving on so well. I'm so sorry."

I could see tears forming in the corners of her eyes, I knew she was genuinely sorry, she was in her own way just trying to look out for me and I couldn't stay mad at her for that. After all the things I had said about Alex after we broke up and the way both my parents had seen me hurting, it doesn't surprise me that she kept the letters a secret. I think I would have probably done the same if I was in her shoes.

"It's okay mum, I know you're just looking out for me. I

need to get to work right now though so I'll see you tonight okay?"

"Okay sweetheart, I love you, again I'm really sorry."

"I love you too mum. No hard feelings, I promise." I quickly gave my mum a kiss on the cheek and shouted up to my brother as I left. I had automatically stuffed the letters into my bag, I had no idea why it's not like I'd get chance to read them at work, come to think of it nor would I have wanted to because no doubt it would bring everything back up for me. The last thing I wanted was to get upset at work again, it certainly wasn't professional.

A part of me felt like I needed to keep them with me so they didn't go missing. My day at work went so slow. All I could think about was those letters, what would they say? Should I open them? Would I be given an explanation as to why she broke my heart or maybe how unbelievably sorry she was? The more and more I tortured myself with the possibilities of what the letters might say, the less I wanted to read them. It had been such a long time since I last spoke to Alex, even longer since I last saw her. There I was finally starting to move forward, I had gotten to the point were I only thought about her a two or three times a day. I felt I had made so much progress, did I really want to risk going back to the beginning? I had exhausted every option by the time it got to 6 pm. I would normally work later on a Monday, I usually have a lot to catch up on from the weekend, but I couldn't bring myself to function any longer. As soon as the clock hand stroked 6 pm, I was putting on my coat and practically running out the door.

It took me a mere twenty minutes to get home, as I pulled up the driveway I could see both my parents were already there. I knew they would be ready with questions about how my day had been, what had I been doing, would I like any dinner etc. As selfish as it may sound I wasn't ready to exchange nicety's and seem just as interested in their day as they were in mine, I just wanted to be alone. I wanted to go to my room and prepare myself for whatever was inside those dreaded letters.

"Hey, how was your day honey?"

The same questions my mum would ask every single day, usually I would tell her all about it with such enthusiasm, today I didn't have it in me.

"Hey Mum…..Hey Dad……it was okay thank you, I'm just grabbing a drink then I'm going to head up to my room, it's been a long day I think I just want to be alone for a little while."

I could tell they both understood straight away, there was no prying. They had always been good at giving me my space, had I ever needed it and today was no different.

"Okay sweetie, do you want me to plate you up some dinner? Me and your dad are having spaghetti bolognaise, there's enough for you too?"

My mum's eyes were searching mine as she spoke, looking for any signs as to how I was feeling about the whole letter situation. My mother was the one person who had always been able to read me like a book.

"No thanks mum, I'm not that hungry."

I grabbed a can of 7UP from the fridge, gave both my parents a reassuring smile and headed upstairs. My mind was in overdrive, it had felt like a week had passed since earlier that morning. I was finally alone in my room, laid on my bed with three letters in my hand. I hadn't told anyone else about the letters. I would eventually tell Whitney and maybe I'd tell Lara, but right now my head was fighting with my heart as to whether I should even open them at all.

After analysing the situation all day, I could only think of one thing in that moment, as clear as day my mind was telling me maybe this is your closure. I didn't know of any other way I could truly get closure from my relationship with Alex, I didn't know if I'd ever see her again, if we would be able to talk it through or even If I'd want to for that matter. This to me seemed the easiest way to finally move on, if I were to read what she had to say maybe then I could close that chapter of my life for good. I guess I hoped it would be that easy, but from my own experience nothing ever was.

I took out the first letter, it was only an A4 sheet of paper with just the front covered. I tried to focus my eyes as tears started to form. Here goes nothing.

Kacy,

Why have you stopped contacting me? I can't understand what I have done wrong, please explain to me, at least give me a call so I can talk to you and find out what it is that's happened. I lost my mobile phone, at least I thought I had lost it, turns out it had been at Jennifer's house, the night that she had the party, I'm sure I told you about that? She found it about 5 days later and I had no messages from you, I had no phone calls. I was worried so I called your mobile, but it went straight to voicemail. Have you changed your mobile number? I thought I had your house phone number, but I must not have saved it, so I didn't know how else to contact you. I did text Whitney but she just told me to leave you alone. I'm so confused Kacy? I miss you so much, I need to hear your voice. Please contact me as soon as you get this letter, my number is still the same. I love you Kacy, don't you every forget that.

Forever yours

A

I didn't know what to make of the letter at first. Why had I stopped contacting her? She was the one that went distant with me. She had lost her phone? Was that just an excuse? Was she just trying to worm her out of it? But that did explain why Jennifer answered her phone, the party also explained the reason she would have been at Jennifer's house the night before. The way Jennifer had said it though made it sound like Alex had been there on her own, just those two. What didn't make any sense to me was that she said her phone had been lost for about five days, that's when it turned up at Jennifer's house? Then why had she answered the phone to me the following day after the party, but only gave Alex her phone back five days later?

Something wasn't right, I didn't know whether to believe Alex's innocence or to disregard the letter all together, it could have just been a last attempt to try and protest her innocence. Whether I didn't trust Alex or I didn't trust Jennifer (which was becoming slightly more likely), I had a lot of figuring out to do. I would have to check with Whitney at some point about the text she received from Alex, it was something she had never mentioned to me.

My heart was torn, breathing became that little bit harder. I had to pull myself back together, there was still two more letters to read, after the first one I assumed they wouldn't be full of apologies or reasons why she had broken my heart, instead I had a gut wrenching feeling that they wouldn't be filled with the answers I was looking for. More than likely they would be filled with the answers that Alex was looking for. I carefully peeled away the edges of the second letter, my hands were trembling. I was finding it more and more difficult to keep my composure. It was almost impossible to keep my stomach working in any sort of normal pattern, like every other part of my body, it clearly had no idea what kind of emotion it should be feeling.

I unravelled two pieces of A4 paper, this letter looked slightly longer than the last. I stared at the first line and took a deep breath before I delved into the unknown.

Kacy,

No reply? It's been almost 4 weeks since I last heard anything from you and I cannot understand what I ever did wrong. I thought we had something special, I thought you loved me in the same uncontrollable, inevitable way that I loved you. I believed with all my heart that you were my soul mate, that even the separation wouldn't harm us or tear us apart. I guess I was wrong. I just wish you would call me, I wish you would contact me in anyway and let me know why you all of a sudden went cold on me.

Did I do something wrong? Was the long distance too hard for you? Because it was for me too, but all you had to do was talk to me about it. I keep beating myself up about anything and everything, wondering what I could have done differently. I know that we didn't talk as much in the last few days because you were busy with work, and I was so busy looking after Rose but that didn't mean for one second I wasn't thinking about you. It's not been easy, I wanted to catch a plane to come and see you to figure all this out, but I couldn't leave her, her health has deteriorated the past week, this happened before at the beginning so I'm hoping she will turn it around. It's so difficult being around the person you love knowing that one day soon they will be gone forever. To watch them slowly fade away and know there's nothing you can do to help is utterly heart-breaking.

I really need you Kacy. A part of me thought maybe you had found someone else and that broke my heart more than you could imagine. I hope that isn't the case but the more and more I don't hear from you, I feel it's better for me to believe that so I can move on. I don't want to move on, but I have no idea what else to do. Every day I think about you, I wonder where you are and what you're doing. I just hope that you are happy. I imagined that I would be the one making you happy, but if that can't be then I wish you every success in everything you do, I truly mean that. If this is it for us, I just wish that I had more days with you, I wish I could have done everything on this earth with you that for me would have been the true definition of happiness. I'll check the post everyday now for the next week hoping that you will find it in you to reply to me so we can figure this out. Even if it's just to tell me what went wrong, I need some form of an explanation I don't think I can ever really recover if I don't receive that from you. Please Kacy surely you can give me that?

I miss you so much

Alex

As I turned the letter over, there was one sentence alone scribbled at the bottom of the piece of paper, it read.

Whatever you do today & everyday of your life, just remember one thing......I will always love you.

The lone sentence she used to finish off every letter we wrote to one another tipped me over the edge. I couldn't control the tears anymore, I finally let them fall down my face with ease as the sudden realisation that I had been wrong came to the forefront of my mind. I had always believed that a part of me had been harsh in cutting Alex from my life the way that I did but I also believed I wasn't the type to be taken for a fool, I wouldn't let someone hurt me that way.

Now I couldn't contain the nauseating feeling as I put down the second letter, had I really been wrong? Had I jumped to conclusions without so much as waiting for an explanation from Alex?

I had always followed my head in situations like that never my heart because I thought your head was always the reasonable one, the one that would prevent further heartbreak in the future so I had gone with my first instinct, I had assumed the worse straight away and never left any room to be convinced otherwise.

I had never had so many doubts in my mind, I could've thrown away the best thing in my life for nothing, for a complete misunderstanding and that for me was just too much to bare.

I was so drained, so tired and lost. I needed to sleep more than anything I needed to shut my eyes and switch off but I simply couldn't think of anything other than the third letter. I had to bring myself to open it, even though I already knew the outcome, I knew she hadn't gotten the reply she was hoping for therefore I almost knew word for word what that letter would say. It would be her final goodbye. With every ounce of strength I had left, I tore open the last letter and just like clockwork the tears came again.

Kacy,

I now sadly have my answer. I haven't been able to sleep for the past week. I guess it's because a part of me knows that it's really over between us now. All I can seem to think of is that the last time I kissed you, I never thought it would be a goodbye kiss or the last time I heard your voice and told you goodnight, I never thought it would be the last time. I want you to know I have no hard feelings, there will be no harsh exchange of words or bitterness from me because you see I love you and a part of me will always love you and if one day we meet again I hope to see you happy, I hope to see that you have achieved everything you set out to and more. I'll remember you with a smile on my face, I will cherish the memories for they are the best ones I have to keep. What we had was real, it was a love that changed my life and right now as I say goodbye I know that there is a good side to what I write today, it means I can start a new beginning and hopefully create a better ending. I have come to terms with moving on now, I know in my heart it is the best thing to do this doesn't mean I will not miss you it doesn't mean I will stop loving you it just means I have to pull myself together and remember a saying that you yourself truly believe in 'everything happens for a reason'.

Take care of yourself Kacy,

Goodbye,

Alex

That was it, a short letter with so much meaning and conviction it was truly heart breaking. She had poured her heart out in three letters and I had replied to none. I was so caught up in my own heartbreak that I never for one second thought about what Alex could be going through, granted I believed she was the bad person in all of this but now how could I not feel differently?

There was one thing I knew about Alex, she wasn't a liar. If what I believed had been true she wouldn't have kept up the façade for all this time. She would have eventually come out with the truth, she would have known why I had cut her from my life and she would have apologised countless times. Instead she hadn't done any of those things from what it seemed she had no idea what had gone wrong. I didn't know what or who to believe, I had convinced myself I had done the right thing. My friends and my family backed me up on that but they only knew what I told them.

As far as I was concerned I had several options, the first one being that I would reply to Alex's letter telling her everything. The second being that I would get her number from Whitney seen as I myself had deleted it and give her a call or a text, and the third option, I would pretend the three letters didn't exist. Instead I would go back to believing what I originally thought, meaning I could continue to move on with my life. The latter being the option I would find hardest to follow through.

It was too late and I was too exhausted to think about the decisions I had to make, the next day I needed to talk to Whitney, she always knew what to say. I could show her the letters and get her take on everything.

I also needed to speak to Lara, whatever was happening between us would almost definitely need to take a back seat. Then there was my parents, well I knew I would be bombarded with questions about what the letters said to begin with. Right then all I wanted was to crawl into bed and let my dreams take me away from the present and what would occur the next day. So that's exactly what I did.

CHAPTER SEVEN

"What do you mean you think you got it wrong? Kacy what's happened?" the familiar sound of Whitney, almost hyperventilating through the phone, was how I spent my lunch hour the next day at work. I had text her almost immediately when I woke up, I didn't have chance to check my phone for the first few hours, but once it got to lunch I had 4 missed calls and 3 messages. "Can I explain everything to you after work? Meet me at my house? I could really use your advice."
I wouldn't have had enough time to eat my lunch whilst trying to explain every minor detail to Whitney.
"Sure anything you want, but I don't think I can wait that long! What time should I come?"
"I finish around 6 so 7 should be fine, if that's okay with

you?" that gave me chance to get home and grab something to eat.

"Perfect, I'll see you then. Just keep it together, love you."

"I love you too, see you later."

I didn't want to get in to much detail at work, the last thing I wanted was to get upset, so I was happy when the phone line went silent. Underneath Whitney's mass of missed calls was also one from Lara, I hadn't spoken to her for almost two days and that was unusual for us as of late. I didn't want to explain to her everything that had happened recently, I didn't even know myself what I was going to do about it all, so the less people that knew, I thought would be better. I quickly sent her a text telling her everything was fine and I had some things to explain to her in the next few days, other than that I had nothing more to say. I didn't want to arrange the next time I would see her until I figured out where I stood with Alex. I felt that may be rather inappropriate. I knew she would understand when the time came.

The rest of the day flew by, I kept myself busy, anything to take my mind off those letters. The people in my office could tell I wasn't my usually chirpy self, but I imagine they would just put it down to having an off day or menstrual cramps, I certainly wasn't about to explain the real reason. When I got home just after 6 pm Whitney was already waiting. I felt nervous when I saw her, I knew that a long talk was in order, a lot of questions would be asked and I had prepared myself as best I could. My parents weren't home so there was no quick greetings needed, we headed straight upstairs to my bedroom, and as soon as Whitney took a seat on my bed I lay all 3 letters out in front of her.

"So that's them, they're in order the one on the left was sent a week after it ended, the next one was a few weeks after that and the last a week after, according to my mum."

"Okay so I'm going to read these first, then I'll know exactly what you need to do, we'll figure this out I promise." She flicked off her $100 sandals and crossed her legs as she began what felt to me like a lifetime of reading. I had been into the bathroom to get changed, tied my hair up out of my face, I'd even been downstairs and made a snack but when I arrived back upstairs, Whitney was still reading.

"Seriously? I know you're a fast reader, what's taking you so long?" clearly she could see the puzzled expression written across my face.

"Girl, I've read them twice over already, I'm just making sure I don't miss any details. So let me get this straight," Whitney meant business, she placed the letters down and looked directly towards me as she began her very lawyer like explanation "you believed Alex was cheating on you with Jennifer, the phone call she answered and the fact that Alex never got back to you in the few days after made that an almost certainty in your mind. Okay, so you deleted her number, you broke off all contact with her, but you never gave her a chance to explain any of the above. She clearly either has no idea why you did what you did or she's a very good liar, I would go for the former on that one. I didn't know Alex the way that you did, but I met her enough times to know she loved you and she was good for you. I didn't believe she would hurt you, but you yourself were so convinced I never questioned anything, hence why when Alex sent me the text message I replied the way I did. Now if you'd of taken my advice about confronting this Jennifer *bitch* this may have been resolved earlier. My conclusion is Alex never cheated on you, I think we have a snake to contend with and I believe that is Jennifer. Maybe she likes Alex, maybe she was jealous of the fact she had a girlfriend, therefore did everything she could to sabotage the relationship, including making it sound like she was meeting Alex alone and not giving Alex her phone back until days later, knowing that you would have assumed the worse by then. Either that or Alex really is a deceitful cow and she's lying in these letters to try and worm her way out of it. In my honest opinion I hate to break it to you babe, but I think this could have been one huge misunderstanding."

Whitney took a breath and sat back, arms folded like she

had just won a battle in a courtroom. That is why I needed her, you could give her anything and she would analyse it in minutes and come back to you with a full blown conclusion, more often than not she was usually right.

"I feared you might say that, what am I going to do Whit? If we believe what we know to be true about Alex and I give her the benefit of the doubt, if I take full responsibility for a stupid mistake I made how will I ever fix this? It's been almost three months since I last spoke to her, I don't think anyone could forgive that." I held my head in my hands, utter disbelief written across my face.

"Alex isn't just anyone, she was or is still the love of your life. I think you need answers Kacy. I think you need to talk to her and find out exactly why it went wrong, explain to her everything you felt, explain about Jennifer and see what her reaction is. You will be able to tell straight away I'm sure. I know this must be difficult for you, but you have a chance to make it right. I think you should go and see her this weekend, it's not something that should be done over the phone. Besides I'm almost positive I deleted her number. Maybe I'm wrong, but if I was Alex and I was in fact innocent in this I would be pretty upset and pissed off at you right now, just the same way that you was with her." she had a point.

"Do you really think I should go? It's so far away though, what if I get there and she doesn't want to see me?

Wouldn't it be better to just write to her? I think I still have her address somewhere....I can't go there alone."
I was slowly breaking down, the tears started to roll down my cheeks yet again.

"Then I'll come with you, we can go this weekend, I have nothing planned and I'm sure we can grab a flight that goes early Saturday. I really don't think it's something you should do through a letter, plus it'll be romantic like the movies, that scene when you run into each other's arm after so long apart." Whitney beamed her best smile at me, I couldn't help but laugh at her between the sobs. She would be the only one to think like that, I was so grateful to have her support, I certainly could not have gone all that way on my own not knowing what the outcome might be, but having Whitney beside me made everything easier.

"Thank you so much Whit, I really appreciate it. I'm not so sure how I feel about going out of the blue, but I guess it's better than not going at all?"

"I think you're right there. What are best friends for? You jump, I jump and all that." I gave her the biggest hug I could fathom at that point. I let the rest of the tears spill knowing they wouldn't be the last. It was Tuesday and I had four days to wait until I could fly out to see Alex. Four whole days to prepare exactly what I would say. I believed I only had this one chance to get it right that's if she was willing to forgive me in the first place and assuming of course all the new found evidence happened to be true.

I had almost immediately began to think I was in the wrong. I had dropped all previous assumptions upon reading the letters, and I hadn't really thought about the fact that there was always a slight possibility I could have got it wrong again. I went with my gut feeling as I always did, I weighed up every last shred of evidence and came to the conclusion that, there was no way of truly knowing until I spoke to Alex in person. Whitney was right, plus it was easy to lie over text, it was easy to lie in a letter or even over the phone, but face to face was always so much harder. I had a good knack for telling if someone was lying, the way they looked at the ground or fiddled with something as they spoke, the frequent deep swallowing and nervous sweats. The signs were always there, nobody was a perfect liar, there was always a way to tell.

We spent the rest of the evening looking at flight times and making the necessary travel arrangements. There was more than enough places to choose from in Cannon Beach, Oregon. We decided upon a nice privately run bed and breakfast called the lighthouse inn, it was perfect for what we wanted and cheap enough. The flight down to Oregon was roughly five hours, according to the flight times we would arrive around 1 pm which suited us both just fine. It was a long way to travel for a day or even two days hence why I had never been when Alex moved there, but now it was different. The next morning I had the dreaded conversation with my parents, I had barely spoken two words to them since Monday morning. It wasn't their fault, I wasn't blaming them or holding any sort of grudge, I just wasn't ready. I knew my parents and they would not let anything drop, ever. I would be bombarded with a million different questions that I myself probably didn't even know the answers too, therefore I chose to retreat and hide away, but it was Wednesday now and not only a new morning, but a countdown beginning, only three more nights.

"Morning sweetheart, how are you feeling today?" my mother gave me her award-winning smile, just last month she had spent a whopping $500 on a new teeth whitening formula, I had to admit though her teeth were some of the best I'd ever seen and totally real from back to front. I myself took pride in my teeth, braces for three whole years when I was younger does that to you, it was just one of the many things my mum had us do, "you want to be able to smile and light up a room" she'd say and she certainly did that.

"Morning, I'm fine mum. There is something I need to tell you though." In between sipping at my glass of freshly squeezed orange juice, I tried to get the words out in the right way. Waiting too long caused the concerned parent look on my mums face, I don't know what it is about saying "there's something I need to tell you" I think most parents expect their children to say that they're pregnant, getting married, moving out or something else drastic. I on the other hand had always been the good girl, unlike my brother, he most definitely would be the one saying he'd gotten some girl pregnant. I actually had a running bet going with my aunt on that one.

"Okay, so the letters kind of shed some light on a few things. I may have been wrong, I may have even slightly overreacted to the whole situation. I won't know for sure until I sort it all out and the only way I can do that is by going to see Alex, this weekend....on Saturday…..morning……until Sunday……and Whitney's coming too." The last sentence came out in quick bursts bit by bit as I saw my mums face grow wider with shock, I don't think she expected that one.

"Wow, are you sure you're doing the right thing? You were so certain about what happened with you and Alex, does this mean she's not the person I've recently thought her to be?" by not being the person they all thought her to be I knew exactly what my mum had meant, you see she wasn't one to swear or to bad mouth anyone, but she certainly expressed her opinion on Alex after seeing how hurt I had been.

"I'm doing what I feel is right mum, Whitney agrees she's

gone through everything with me and she thinks going to see Alex and talking it out is going to be the best thing to do. I know it's a long shot, I'm just hoping that I was completely wrong so that I no longer have to waste time hating her and I can go back to what I did best." By the last part I meant going back to loving her, because that's what I did best, it's what I was good at. She made loving her so easy and I missed that.

My mum understood exactly what I meant, and for the most part I think she knew how I must be feeling. They say twins have a sort of twin telepathy, well I think mother and daughter have the same thing.

"Okay honey, I support you in whatever you choose to do you know that. Just remember you have your whole life ahead of you, if things don't work out now they will one day, don't worry."

"I know they will mum, thank you, I love you."

"I love you too sweetheart."

CHAPTER EIGHT

Journal entry:

I know what I have to do now. I haven't written in a while, the past few months have been more than difficult for me. I find it clears my mind and helps put things in perspective when I jot them down. I hope with all my heart that everything works out for the best, I won't sit here and write about how I want to get Alex back and live happily ever after, I'm a realist and I would rather things work out the way they are supposed to, if that means me and Alex were never meant to be then that is reality, that is what was written in the stars and the way It was always going to be.

My mum is a true believer in fate and destiny, I guess I am too in some ways. Some people would say that our life's are already mapped out for us, but I don't believe that because then choice would be taken away, the option to choose what we want, what we will do and who we will be are so important. We have those choices so we can make mistakes, so we can learn and grow as human beings. I chose to love Alex, I chose to leave Alex and now I choose to fly to Oregon to get her back. These are all my choices, but I do like to think that fate & destiny had a little bit to do with how we met and how we will meet again.

I just got off the phone with Whitney we fly out to Oregon tomorrow, the day has finally arrived. I'm incredibly nervous, more so because a part of me doesn't know what to expect or how she may react. I never really thought about her ignoring me completely, which let's be honest would be a certain possibility. I may have gotten everything, let's just say a little mixed up.

I knew Alex to be an understanding person, but I may have overstepped the mark slightly. Anyway that's enough speculating from me, my head hurts with the amount of times I keep changing my mind. I need to talk to Lara, before I forget, I'll do that now.

Lara Grey-Whitely wasn't a person you easily forgot about. I had so much on my mind, I had forgotten to reply to the slowly growing stream of text messages. She didn't bombard me or get angry because I had become distant of late. She simply wanted to check I was okay, she asked if I needed anything or someone to talk to, on more than one occasion, that was the person she was, totally selfless and beautiful not just outside, but also in. Her soul was pure and that was rare these days, she genuinely was such a nice person, I wanted to keep her a part of my life, whether that would be possible in the future I didn't know. I decided to place that in the barrel of questions yet unanswered.

I knew one thing though, I loved her. Not in the way I loved Alex, that was an undeniable epic love, but I did love her, it was just different. People wouldn't have understood, if anyone asked me to explain it I don't think I could. They say you can't be truly in love with two people at once, but I definitely think you can love two people differently at the same time.

Sometimes I think you just meet someone and it's so clear on some level that you belong together, whether that's as lovers or as friends or as something entirely different, that's how I feel about Lara, we just work, we understand one another. I knew from then on it would be a bond I would always have with her.

I didn't want to reply over text it was too disrespectful and impersonal for the type of conversation I would have with her. It was 9 pm and I flew out to Oregon at 6 in the morning, I certainly felt it was time to tell her everything, the last thing I wanted was her finding out from somebody else.

"Hey Kacy, finally you call."

"Lara, I'm so sorry. I've been so busy and my minds been a little distracted as of late, I promise I haven't been ignoring you."

"Don't worry about it, as long as you're okay? Do you want to tell me what's been on your mind?"

I did want to tell her, the hardest part was how to put it, I didn't quite feel comfortable pouring my heart out like I would to Whitney, mainly because I knew Lara had feelings for me just as I did for her.

"I'm okay I guess, I don't really know how to explain it, basically a few days ago my mum gave me some letters, three all together, they were from Alex. The last one had been sent about a month ago."

I took a deep breath and listened as the line remained

silent. I was waiting for a response, anything at all. Finally about ten seconds later I got it.

"Oh okay, go on what did they say?" Reluctantly I went ahead and explained the contents of the three letters, she didn't need to hear all the details, especially not anything remotely romantic. I had to bear in mind the relationship I had with Lara, I didn't want to make that any more awkward than it was at that moment.

"And you believe everything she's said? I mean you know her better than I do so I trust your instinct."

"I think so, Whitney's seen the letters too and she thinks I could of got it wrong, I mean her story does kind of add up, the only thing I question is Jennifer."

"I agree I think if Alex didn't cheat on you then that Jennifer girl sure wanted it to seem that way. So what are you going to do?"

The line went silent on my end, she had been so cool and calm throughout my explaining of the whole situation. I was worried that would soon turn.

"Well I kind of made a split second decision the other night.........I'm flying out to Oregon tomorrow morning. Whitney's coming too."

"Okay....I.." I cut her off immediately to explain.

"It's just something I need to do, I hope you understand. I think a part of me needs clarity and closure, I need to know what really happened in order to move forward. What's been happening with us I just want you to know it meant something to me, I can't explain it I just want you to know that I'm not trying to hurt you, that's the last thing I want."

"What I was going to say was that I think you're doing the right thing. You need this just like you said, I know you're not trying to hurt me and you haven't, we both knew what this was, if it turns out to be more in the future then we will deal with that, but right now you need to figure out some things. If Alex isn't the bad guy after all then I know that any sort of future with us is very unlikely, but I'm okay with that Kacy. I'm here for you if you need me no matter what, there will be no hard feelings, I promise you that."

I had to stop myself from crying not because I was sad, but because I knew how amazing Lara was, she had such a kind heart. A part of me felt at a loss that I hadn't kept her in my life longer after we broke up a few years back, even just as friends, she had fast become one of the best people I knew.

"Thank you so much Lara, It makes me so happy to know you understand and support me."

"Of course, just promise me one thing?"

"Anything."

"Don't feel like you have to keep things from me, you can tell me anything, anytime of the day. If nothing more I at least want to be here for you as your friend. Also if you and Alex don't work out then you call me up

because I'll be here waiting for that second chance."
We both couldn't help but giggle at the last comment, she was trying to lighten the mood as she always did, but I knew deep down she meant it. What I said next even surprised me.

"I love you Lara." As easy as if I was saying hello the words flowed from my mouth with ease. Her response as apparent and true ended our conversation.

"I love you too K."

It was 3 am on Saturday morning, my previous night's sleep had been very much disturbed. I must have woken up on the hour every hour, bearing in mind I had gotten off the phone with Lara just after 10 pm so my total sleep combined was at best three hours. The plan was for me to pick Whitney up at 3:30 am and head straight to the Airport, which would give us enough time to check in and grab some breakfast before the flight. The flight was definitely what I was looking forward to most, simply because it was five hours long and I knew I'd be able to top up my rough night's sleep.

There had only been first class available on the day we booked, but I was grateful for the extra legroom and reclining seats despite the hefty price tag. I would've certainly paid anything to get a little sleep and not look like a complete Zombie at that particular moment. Everything ran smoothly from arriving at the pre-paid car park, to check in, to security and passport control. It was plain sailing, no bag searches or body searches, no queue a mile long with frustrated passenger's "tutting" at every person who bleeped walking through the metal detectors, I think it was my lucky day. I even had a quick chat to the girl behind the coffee bar, when she stated that the coffee was on her my confidence boosted automatically, I'd had three hours sleep, I was dressed in my comfy clothes with my hair scraped back and I still had it.

"Look at you grinning, I guess she didn't think you looked bad at all." Whitney walked off giggling to herself making it more than obvious to the cashier that we were In fact talking about her.

I was trying my best to stop overanalysing everything. I knew having Whitney with me would take my mind of most things, I started to think of it as a girly weekend away and if I happened to bump into Alex whilst I was there, well I would deal with that at the time. It was the only way I could calm myself.

Every time I thought about anything to do with Alex or the situation I was currently in, I told myself that I will only live once and everything happened for a reason. Yes, they are two complete clichés, but they always seemed to make me feel better when I said them, they gave a sort of understanding as to why we do the things we do.

The flight went as smooth as can be, the free on board

meal went down a treat. I don't know what it was about plane food that I loved so much, but a nice warm ham and cheese Panini at 9 in the morning was certainly a good way to start the day. Like I had hoped, I slept for three hours. Luckily for me there wasn't any screaming children keeping me awake in first class, I heard the faint tapping of laptop keys from the woman behind me clearly on a business trip, but once the engines set off roaring that sound soon faded away.

Whitney was slightly more prepared than I was, she had a small green make-up style bag, inside the contents included one set of ear plugs, some hard boiled sweets and a gorgeous super soft cotton eye mask.

It was about an hour before landing when I awoke from a rather disturbed sleep, although surprisingly not as bad as the night before. Whitney was already awake and reading the latest GQ magazine, predominantly seen as a men's magazine, but she loved to read it anyway. Sometimes the likes of Rihanna and Megan Fox would grace the front cover, she hoped one day it would be her face lined up on shelves across millions of stores. The girl had ambition.

"Hey, how did you sleep?"

"Okay I guess, not as well as you with your ear plugs though. I need to remember that for next time. How far away are we?"

"I think about 55 minutes, we should start descending

soon, are you nervous?" I was in a way I think it was only normal, but I was never the type to get so worked up and uneasy. I knew that when I came face to face with her all the fear would fade away almost instantly.

"A little I guess, I'm trying not to think too much into it."

"God I'd be all over the place if I was you, you're always so much cooler than me in situations like this."

"I don't think we've ever been in a situation like this Whit." I laughed a little too out loud.

"Yes I guess not, anyway you know what I mean. So what's the plan of action once we land?" I wish I had a straightforward answer for her, but I honestly hadn't thought that far ahead.

"I think first we need to grab a taxi to our hotel, then we can check in put our stuff away and figure out where Alex is staying. I have the address written down from when I used to send letters, but we'll need to ask for directions." Whitney nodded along with everything I said, she knew I'd be taking the reins on this one she was just there for support.

"Sounds good to me, but first port of call, we need food. Isn't town only five minutes away from the hotel? We can go there first and find somewhere to eat."

"You read my mind." I was so hungry.

The security and passport control in Oregon was just as smooth as North Carolina, it seemed someone was looking down on me. I hoped the good fortune would continue. We didn't need to wait for our baggage as we only had hand luggage for the short one night stay. All in all it took a quick twenty minutes to get through the airport and out the other side, the weather was quite warm for that time of year, no rain or wind which I was grateful for. A taxi certainly wasn't hard to find, a line of twenty cabs were already ready and waiting, we jumped in the first one available to us.

"Hi, Cannon beach please, the lighthouse inn."

"Certainly my love, in current traffic it'll take 30 minutes to get there." Said the cheerful cab driver, I'd say he was around 50 years old, but he was very good looking for his age.

"Thank you, that's fine." The cab driver didn't have much to say on the journey which I was thankful for, me and Whitney had so much to talk about that the thirty minutes felt like five. We pulled up outside the Lighthouse Inn at around 12:45 in the afternoon, it looked lovely from the outside, although it didn't look like a standard hotel it looked like a very large mansion with several balconies spread across two floors.

We were promptly shown to our room on arrival, we had booked the Queen suite as it happened to be the only one available at the time, and everything from the décor, to the TV, to the balcony was very well presented. We had our very own private kitchenette, a small living area which consisted of a plush cream sofa sat opposite a large screen television, and a king size bed at the other side of the room. It was nicely decorated throughout with a consistent cream and purple theme, I started to envy people that had the pleasure of staying here for longer than one evening. This was certainly a place I'd come to again. I dropped my carry on at the door and sprawled out across the bed, comfortable was an understatement.

I soon realised there was only one bed, but that didn't bother either of us, we often shared my bed when Whitney stayed over at my house. I quickly had to remind myself why we had come, I could have easily gotten swept up in the beautiful ways of Cannon beach, but unfortunately the trip wasn't intended for that. Whitney placed the hotel telephone back in its cradle after a quick conversation with the hotel reception.

"So I asked the receptionist to call us a cab, she said it would be about ten minutes. Are you ready to head out?"

"Yeah let's do this, I need something to eat."

"Have you thought about where you can find Alex? Do you think she has a job in town somewhere?" The thought had crossed my mind, but from what I could remember Alex's grandma Rose had quite a lot of money saved up, which in turn would mean Alex didn't have to work. The whole point of her coming out here was to look after Rose and help her enjoy the life she had left.

"I doubt it, but honestly I wouldn't know. Anything could have changed since I last spoke with her."

"I guess so, anyway lets go the cab should be here any minute." It only took a short five minute cab drive into the small town, it was a nice close knit community similar to where I used to live in Hyde County, which wasn't something I'd experienced in a number of years. Choosing somewhere to grab something to eat was a task in itself, for a small town there was more than enough coffee shops and cafés, every other shop posed a new option for us both.

After walking for a few minutes we settled on a small family run café called the Lazy Susan Café. The name was rather unusual, but that just intrigued me more. Whitney like myself was a huge waffle fan so the first thing on the menu was ordered instantly, the oatmeal waffle delight. It was by far the most amazing waffle I'd ever tried, such a beautiful presentation with an array of fruits topped off with whipped cream and chocolate sauce. I was in heaven. Conversation began to flow whilst we ate.

"So what time do you think you want to go and see Alex?"

"Well I guess I need to go soon, we only have a day here so I can't leave it too late, the more I think about just turning up on her doorstep the more nervous I get. I can't imagine what her reaction is going to be."

"I know Hun I would be crazy nervous right now, but I'm

here for you all the way. I can go back to the hotel if you like or come along it's up to you, although I don't wish to be a third wheel." Whitney winked as she devoured the remainder of her waffle.

"I want you to come, but I think it's something I need to do on my own. I'm pretty sure where she lives is only a few minutes away from here, over that way somewhere," I pointed towards the back of the Café "you could always hang around town, there's plenty of shops to explore?" Whitney's eyes lit up before me, clearly the idea of shopping had perked her up, she was the ultimate queen of shopping and nothing suited her better than small town boutiques.

"Oooh good idea K, did you see that beautiful boutique on the way in? The dress in the window, I need it, that's what I'll do. You take your time I'm sure there's enough shops here to keep me busy for a few hours." I wasn't worried about leaving her in the slightest I knew she would actually prefer to shop than sit back at the hotel. We finished up at the café and made our way back onto the main street. The hustle and bustle I was used to in Raleigh wasn't quite the same here. As you would expect most places were busy on a Saturday afternoon, but here it was just nice, it was bearable and not quite the run of the mill tourist place I would've expected. I could see almost immediately why Rose would have loved the place so much, I imagined Alex would have settled there just fine also. I walked Whitney back towards the boutique and gave her a quick hug goodbye before I set off in the opposite direction.

"Good luck honey, call me when you're done."

"Thanks Whit, I will do, see you later."

The Cab had dropped us off earlier that day outside the Taxi Rank so I immediately retraced my steps back to that same place. It may have only been a ten minute walk, but I didn't know the area and the last thing I needed was to get lost. As I wondered down the half empty street I contemplated turning around on more than one occasion, but what my heart wanted always prevailed and what it wanted was Alex. That I knew with every inch of my being so I owed it to myself to try, to at least see the positives in a situation that at first seemed to be so negative.

How the tides had changed since earlier that week, the girl I loved, the girl I had fallen so deeply in love with had hurt me in a way I had never been hurt before. My heart had been broken into what felt like a million tiny pieces. I felt as though piecing them back together was impossible. I had clinched onto every last hope when I read the letters because I still wasn't over her, she had touched my soul in such a way that I could physically nor mentally remove her from it. What would I do if everything I had come to believe was true? If the new found hope I had was suddenly shattered, that's when reality would surely hit me like a ton of bricks, but that was a chance I was willing to take. I had not come this far to turn back now, my thoughts exactly.

Then I saw her.

CHAPTER NINE

Have you ever felt everything and nothing all at the same time? It is an indescribable experience. To feel every crack of your heart, but at the same time feel so numb that you're not even sure it's really happening. To hold little pockets of hope and then suddenly have each and every one of them ripped from your grasp as though they never existed. What I saw then made everything real, it brought everything back to the surface as if it was happening right in that moment, as if she was still mine and now she was with her. I had placed too much faith in something I couldn't control and for that I would pay the ultimate price.

I realised after a minute that I had simply frozen, I had given no signal to my body to move in anyway shape or form. I was in plain sight of Alex, I could see her and another woman together. Only they weren't together with Rose or with Natalie, they were alone, hands entwined strolling down the street as though they had no care in the world. I could only assume that the woman was in fact Jennifer. I had been right all along. I wanted to run, as far away from Cannon beach until my legs gave out and I could no longer stand, but I still couldn't move. I had no choice but to continue to observe my ultimate nightmare. I just wished I could've woken up.

What struck me was the way Alex held Jennifer at a distance, she didn't seem happy to be showing the public displays of affection that Jennifer was so willingly throwing her way. It was a mental picture far different from the way we used to be together. The two looked to be shopping, I watched them enter a small boutique about five stores down from where I was stood, but on the opposite side of the road. The boutique looked familiar, the dress in the beautifully displayed window in particular. Then it struck me that was the boutique Whitney had been so eager to enter only ten minutes earlier. I wanted to turn and leave, if Alex saw Whitney she would know I was there. That would be a complete disaster. My mind was so clouded I could barely thing what to do next, my first instinct was to call Whitney and tell her to leave the boutique. I fumbled around in my pocket for my phone and immediately hit the first number on speed dial.

"Hey Kacy, everything okay?" Thank god she answered on the third ring.

"Whitney you need to get out of that boutique like now, Alex has just entered with Jennifer, I'll explain later but we need to leave." I tried my best not to sound so panicked, but every word that exited my mouth sounded so high-rate.

"Omg slow down, okay I'm just in the changing room trying on a dress, I don't know how I'll get around them, this place isn't exactly huge." Whitney's voice lowered to just above a whisper.

"Well you'll have to wait in the changing room until their gone."

"I can't there's only one changing room in here and there'll be a queue of people…..she might be one of them."

"Then you'll have to make something up tell them you're here on business if they spot you…I don't know what else to say." I was getting myself more and more worked up, all I wanted was for the world to open up and swallow me under so I didn't have to live through this any longer.

I watched on whilst speaking to Whitney on the phone, I couldn't see clearly from across the street the suns glare was bouncing off the windows, which meant I couldn't give Whitney any insight as to their whereabouts inside the store. From what I could gather the single fitting room was at the rear right of the boutique, and the till at the left, to get to the exit you had to walk straight through the centre clearly visible to everyone around.

"Okay I'll try my best just sit tight, I'll be out soon. Wait! Where are you?"

"I'm across the street down the alleyway. Hurry." With that the line went dead, all I could hope was that Whitney would get out unseen. I didn't want a show down with Alex and Jennifer at this point, I had been right all along and the worse thing was I had given myself hope, I had believed everything she wrote in those letters. I must have had stupid written across my forehead.

Suddenly the realisation hit me, it wasn't that I regretted the past because what me and Alex had was undeniable, it was memories I would never forget and a love I would always remember, but what I did regret was the lost future, a future that we would never have, memories that would never be made and a love that would fade, and be no more.

I did wonder if she felt she had made a mistake or if I had been just as dispensable to her as anyone else. I had time to ponder over everything whilst the minutes dragged out. Whitney eventually came bounding out of the front door of the boutique. My heart sank for a moment until I realised nobody was following her, she did it.

"You got away without them seeing you?"

"Not quite." Whitney took a moment to catch her breath.

"What do you mean?" slight panic reappeared in my voice.

"Alex saw me, well actually that Jennifer bitch turned just as I was passing and I bumped into her. Alex turned to see me and stood shocked for a second, I didn't really know what to say so I just said 'Sorry, gotta go.' And I practically ran from the shop."

"So let me get this straight, Alex could think that I'm here with you too?"

"Well I guess it's a possibility, I'm so sorry honey I didn't want to stick around, if I got talking to her I was afraid I might say some things I'd regret." I peered back around the corner to see across the street, Alex and Jennifer had just left the boutique and headed towards the next shop, they looked to be having a rather heated conversation.

"It's okay I know, let's just get out of here please before they see me."

We arrived back at the Hotel fifteen minutes later, I hadn't been able to talk on the ride back I needed a few minutes to clear my head. Now that we had safely arrived in the room with no prying eyes or ears the questions began.

"So what was that all about? Clearly her and Jennifer are

together now? Do you think she knows you're here? How did you spot her? Did you see what that Jennifer was wearing? I don't like her or her fashion sense."

"Wow slow down, one question at a time seriously. I saw her walking on the opposite side of the road as I was heading to get a cab, she was holding hands with Jennifer and laughing like she didn't have a care in the world. She didn't see me definitely not and I certainly hope she doesn't know where we are. Unless she followed you, but I think there is very little chance of that. In regards to her fashion sense I honestly was too shocked to even take notice." I was trying to stay strong, but holding back tears was becoming a difficult process. Whitney came up and sat beside me on the bed to give me her best friend hug and vote of confidence.

"Look honey she is not worth your tears, she will realise deep down what she's lost and she'll be kicking herself for the rest of her life, but you…..you will move on to bigger and better things….you'll find some gorgeous girl that will make you forget who Alex was because you're gorgeous, sweet, funny and kind. I'll give you time to recover because I know this is hurting you, but then we're going to find you someone worthy. Hey there's always Lara, she seems to be stepping up to the plate lately, don't rule her out will you."

"Thanks Whitney, I love you."

"Love you too honey."

I had thought about Lara in more ways than one lately, I wanted her in my life no matter what whether that was as a friend or more. Only time would tell.

A few hours passed, we ordered room service for Dinner as I didn't want to leave the hotel for fear of bumping into Alex. It was 6 pm, only another twenty four hours before we could get our fight back to Raleigh. I wished time would speed up, there was only so much daytime TV and room service I could deal with. I hadn't brought any books or any work with me or even my laptop because I hadn't exactly predicted the outcome that had arisen.

I returned from getting a glass of water from the kitchenette, to my surprise the phone started ringing. I assumed it must be the hotel reception.

"Hello."

"Hello Miss Sullivan, your guest is here at reception, would you like me to send them up to your room?"

"I'm sorry, but I'm not expecting a guest could you ask them who it is please?" at this point Whitney had entered the room, quizzing eyes looking my way.

"Miss Alex Dawson, she asks for you to join her in the lobby." I slammed the phone back down on the receiver as I slumped onto the bed. I couldn't breathe, how did she know I was here, why had she come to see me, to humiliate me some more?

"Whitney its Alex, she's at reception, she wants to see me."

"Do you want me to go and tell her to leave?"

Whitney would certainly do a little more than tell her to leave, I didn't want her to cause a scene in the middle of the hotel lobby that could easily have us removed.

"I think I need to face her don't I? I don't want to cower away like some scared, heartbroken, little girl anymore. She obviously knows I'm here, I can't give her the satisfaction of knowing I'm hurting. I refuse to do it anymore."

"That's my girl, don't you back down, don't let her see you cry, go down there and tell her she's made the biggest mistake she'll ever make and then walk away with your head held high."

That's exactly what I planned to do, luckily for me I hadn't taken my make up off, I gave myself a quick check over in the mirror, added a touch of hairspray and a squirt of my favourite Roberto Cavalli perfume, before heading to the door.

Whitney called out "Good luck honey." I had never felt my heart pound so fast in my chest, I could feel every thud like it would explode at any moment. I had earlier worried what my reaction would be when I first saw her, but I had already experienced that only I didn't feel love and hope when I looked upon her, instead I felt hatred and heartbreak, two things I honestly never would have predicted at the beginning.

Now I had to face her again, I walked the long corridor to the lobby taking in the décor I had earlier ignored, each side was neatly decorated with vibrant orange and red designs, vases of flowers were placed on solid wood stands every few metres. Leather lounge chairs filled the lobby as I grew closer, several televisions mounted the walls constantly playing the news/music throughout the day. I took a deep breath as I urged my legs to take the last few strides into the lobby.

Alex was the first thing I saw, she was sat over by the window with her phone in hand, she glanced up as I approached. I must have startled her because she jumped up from her seat and dropped her phone, that didn't bother her though, she left it laying on the floor as she stared at me, almost in a trance. The way she took all of me in from head to toe made me incredibly nervous. After what felt like a lifetime, she finally broke the silence.

CHAPTER TEN

"I didn't think you'd come down, I was going to wait here all night If that's what it took." I gave her no smile or friendly banter, I got straight to the point.

"What do you want Alex?"

"I wanted to see you. Why are you here? Did you come to see me? Why didn't you call me or write back to me Kacy?" The last part was almost a plea, like she had been dyeing to know why for such a long time.

"Don't play dumb with me Alex, I did come here to see you, after I read your letters I was willing to give you the benefit of the doubt, but I soon realised I had made the same mistake twice."

"What are you talking about, give me the benefit of the

doubt? You just stopped talking to me! I didn't know why or what I did." My first thought was that she was clearly trying to play dumb on this one. Why wouldn't she just admit what she'd done? I had witnessed it with my own two eyes that afternoon.

"I stopped talking to you? Alex why won't you just admit that you were cheating on me with Jennifer, it was pretty obvious. You didn't text me back for days and she answered your phone for god's sake Alex, stop lying to me." I watched the confusion spread across Alex's face, if she knew what I was talking about then she was a very good actress. At that point I couldn't stand anymore my legs felt weak so I took a seat across from where Alex was now sitting.

"I never cheated on you Kacy, I would never do that, I loved you too much. I would have never hurt you like that." Then as if something had clicked she said.

"What do you mean she answered my phone?"

"What I said Alex, you said in your letter that you 'lost your phone' well why did Jennifer answer it the next day? She said you'd left it at her house the night before." All this seemed to be breaking news to Alex, I was beginning to think she had no idea what Jennifer had done.

"I swear to you Kacy, I lost my phone, Jennifer didn't give it me back until days later. I went to her house that night with Nat because she was having a house warming party and……Rose told me I should get out of the house. When I finally got my phone back I had no contact from you, your phone went straight to voicemail when I tried to call, I even text Whitney and she told me to leave you alone, I had no idea what I'd done wrong Kacy."

The way she choked up when she said rose's name sent a shiver through me, I didn't want to ask just then, but I feared the worst had already happened.

"How do you explain what I just witnessed in town earlier today then? You and Jennifer? You're clearly an item now."

"It started a few weeks ago, I never had any interest in Jennifer when I was with you Kacy, I swear to you, but you didn't reply to any of my letters, you didn't text me or call me. I was heartbroken for months. Then a few weeks ago I decided it was time to move on and Jennifer was just there, she had been for the past few months. It just happened. Not one day has gone by that I haven't thought about you, more than once I wanted to fly out to Raleigh, but I was too embarrassed at how you just dropped me, I didn't want to show you how hurt I was because I thought that you had obviously found somebody else." I explained my side of the story, I told her why I had stopped speaking to her and I explained every last detail down to the exact words Jennifer had said. I even made a point of reliving every single feeling I had felt over the past three months.

"I'm so sorry for everything Kacy, you have to believe me I would never hurt you. I can't believe I have missed spending the last three months of my life with you because of her. I thought she was a bit too full on from the start, when I told her I had a girlfriend she didn't like it I could tell, I should've known something was off, why she had only found my phone five days after I was there was strange now I think about it."

I could see the guilt in her eyes, I could feel her heartbreak as it mirrored my own. I was completely lost for words, the rollercoaster of emotions I had felt that day started to take its toll. I broke down right there in the main lobby of the hotel, the other guests sauntered by clearly getting an eyeful of the scene unfolding. I wondered what they would be thinking for a second, but soon realised I really did not care.

The tears came thick and fast with no warning, Alex moved closer to my side to comfort me. I felt her arm close around my waist as the other came up to wipe away the tears. I couldn't bring myself to pull away, her touch, the way she smelt so perfectly beside me was intoxicating. I believed her side of the story, I should have known from the beginning, I should have trusted that I knew the person she was; so kind, caring, sweet, protective and loving. She was never the lying, cheating, heartless person I had made myself believe she was. The whole time her heart had been breaking uncontrollably, just like mine. If one thing was certain all along, despite all that had happened, I loved her, I would always love her, which was the one thing certain in my life.

Resting my head upon her shoulder I let the familiar feeling overcome me, the happiness I had not felt in months surrounded me as her arms took me completely in embrace. As soon as my tears started to dry a sudden realisation hit Alex, she darted upright and took off for the door.

"Alex, where are you going?"

"I'm going to see Jennifer, I want an explanation for why she ruined my life. How could she do that? I need to find out."

"Wait...are you going to come back?"

"Of course I will, there's so much we need to catch up on...I'll be back later, I promise."

"Wait.....I love you Alex, I never stopped. I just need you to know that."

"I love you too Kacy, more than you will ever know." Just like that she was gone. I quickly gathered myself and headed for the lift. I had already embarrassed myself enough with the display in the lobby, I didn't need more passers by seeing my mascara streaked face. The mirrors in the lift did not help matters, I looked like a clown from a bad horror movie, I was thankful to not be sharing the lift with any other guests. I made my way down to room number 34, before I had chance to walk through the door, Whitney pounced.

"KACY!! I've been waiting up here pacing around, twiddling my thumbs, biting my nails, what's happened? You were gone for like a week!!" Okay there was a slight exaggeration on the week, clearly Whitney couldn't contain her eagerness to know how the situation had unfolded. She must of eyed my clown like features because she all of sudden went quiet.

"I'm so sorry, are you okay?"

"I'm okay, actually I think everything's going to be just fine." I explained to Whitney word for word what Alex had said, she believed her just like I did, she always trusted my judgement so if I believed her, so would she. We spoke for several hours about expectations now that the truth had come to light, but I myself didn't know. Only time would tell was my best answer.

Whitney like myself quickly took a disliking to Jennifer, the woman that had more or less ruined my relationship and stolen my girlfriend. I wanted to meet this woman, I wanted to see if she had any remorse for what she had done. My first thought was definitely not, why would she? Clearly this was something she was good at, maybe she had a past of stealing girlfriends, of being deceitful and undermining. I just hoped that Alex would see through any lies, no doubt she would deny everything and plead her love for Alex as a bargaining chip, that's what woman like her do, they don't like to lose. I figured it wouldn't be the last time Jennifer became a thorn in my side.

I was on the verge of sleep when the Hotel phone rang, the clock showed 10:32 pm, it had been a long day, my eyes were sore from the obscene amount of crying I had done, sleep had seemed like my only option and by far the best.

"Hello."

"Hello Miss Sullivan, you have a call waiting at reception would you like me to transfer it through to your room?"

"Yes that would be great, Thanks."

"No problem Miss Sullivan, good evening." The phone line Clicked and a new voice appeared on the other end.

"Hi, is that Kacy?" I was expecting Alex, this voice I didn't recognise.

"Yes it is, can I ask who's speaking?" There was silence for a few seconds.

"It's Jennifer, I'm sure you know me by now? Anyway I'll get straight to the point. I want you to leave town tomorrow and never look back, you had your chance with Alex now she's with me and that's how it's going to stay. Whatever little plan you've got in that head of yours will fail, I'll make sure of it. You see there's a difference between me and you, I wouldn't have let the love of my life go as easily as you did, you really didn't put up a fight, I was quite disappointed actually. Whatever you told Alex, has upset her, I don't like it when she's upset, you see she has blamed me for your breakup, she's taken every little word that's come from your mouth and believed it, I'll give you credit for that, but now it's over. She will forgive me in time because she loves me more than she ever loved you, I was there for her when she needed someone, when Rose passed, I was there not you, so please do us all a favour, don't make this harder than it needs to be. Are we clear on that?" I had the phone on loudspeaker so that Whitney could hear the whole conversation, her eyes blazing with fury, I couldn't help but laugh once the conversation had ended on her part. Who was this woman threatening me? I wasn't some pussycat about to roll over and play dead. I took tips from Whitney sat beside me, she was always a fantastic argument winner, she nudged me several times egging me on.

"Listen Jennifer, I know the type of person you are, and well let's just say "Bitch" is an understatement. Alex is only with you because she thought she'd lost me, thanks for that by the way. You are not first choice nor will you ever be, if I leave tomorrow do you think Alex won't follow? What else is keeping her here? God bless Rose, she was the only reason Alex moved to this town, her life and her friends are all in Raleigh, so I'm afraid you don't have a leg to stand on. I don't know what you think you're achieving by calling me, if you think I'm scared of you and your threats you're sincerely mistaken. I'd like to know just one thing, have you always been this crazy?" Whitney couldn't help but laugh at the last comment, I had to stick my hand over her mouth to control the laughter whilst I waited for a reply. The line went dead.

"Well that "Bitch" clearly didn't have a reply to that one did she? What if she turns out to be a serial killer? She did seem just a little crazy." Whitney used hand gestures to show the little, which in actual fact was rather big. She had a point, I didn't know what I was dealing with. The quicker I got out of Cannon Beach the better.

"Let's hope not. Do you remember Sarah Brooks from high school? Jennifer reminds me a lot of her, she went completely off the rails after the first year of college, apparently tried to kill her husband with a screwdriver!"

"Yes I do! What are you going to do now? Call Alex? Obviously she's been to see Jennifer."

"I have no way of contacting her, she changed her number, besides I deleted it so that would be no use anyway. It's late I thought she'd come back here, but I'm sure she'll come through in the morning."

I hoped she would anyway, there was still so much out in the open, so much unresolved. I honestly didn't know where I stood with any of it. Rose must have passed recently, the thought was utterly heart-breaking. A pang of guilt entered my body because I hadn't been there for her, to hold her hand through one of the hardest moments of her life. As heart-breaking as it was it meant there was nothing else keeping her there in Oregon. Alex's apartment and her bar and all her friends where back in Raleigh, it made me question why she had stuck around this long already, was Jennifer keeping her here? Did she actually have real feelings for Jennifer now? I needed answers to my questions and I needed them fast. Eighteen hours remained until our fight departed.

CHAPTER ELEVEN

The alarm on my phone sounded, it was 8 am. I felt like I'd been asleep for minutes not hours. I awoke several times in the night to check my phone thinking I would see a text from Alex, but I soon realised that wasn't possible. My morning routine was well underway when Whitney woke an hour later, Breakfast in the hotel was served between 7 and 10 am. I was told by another guest that it wasn't to be missed. It took Whitney a mere fifteen minutes to get ready, she really was a natural beauty, no make-up required to make her look as amazing as she did. By 9:20 am I was sat around the breakfast table, in the far corner of the canteen room by the window, the view of Cannon beach could be seen perfectly through the mass of trees.

Once we settled with our food, cereal for me and fruit with yoghurt for Whitney, the conversation started to flow.

"Do you think Alex will come this morning?" Whitney just about managed to get out the words, in between the mouthfuls of fruit.

"I hope so, I mean I don't really know, she just said she would be back later. I didn't even have time to tell her I was only here until later this afternoon."

"Well I guess we need to go and find her then, we can pack our stuff and leave them at reception, you have her address right?" I rummaged around in my new rustic brown satchel bag, to find a small piece of paper.

"Here it is, let's hope she's still there." I said with slight concern spread across my face.

"Don't look so worried honey, it'll all work out just fine, I have a good feeling about this, you guys just need some time alone to talk things through, or at least trade phone numbers, unfortunately we are not living in the dark ages anymore K." I laughed and almost choked on a lucky charm.

"You're totally right, exchanging phone numbers is a must. I don't know why, but I'm kind of nervous."

"You don't need to be nervous, you told me last night how easy it felt to be with her again, like no time had passed. That's exactly what it will be like, you still love her right?"

"I'll always love her Whit, I can't explain it. Even though we've been apart for all this time it feels like she's still mine. I definitely never stopped loving her even when I thought the worst of her, that's why I know its true love, it's like nothing I've ever felt before." I smiled at the thought of Alex, of being with her again, nothing made me happier.

"That's so sweet, look at you with that grin on your face, it's so nice to see a genuine smile again. You deserve to be happy Kacy."

"I hope we can be Whit, I really do."

There was a nice silence while we both finished our breakfast, no awkward need to talk, just two best friends happy in the company of one another. The hotel kitchen staff started to clear away the hot breakfast followed by the cereals, then it was time to go. It took no longer than ten minutes to pack our belongings and do one last sweep of the hotel room, we only took the bare minimum for such a short trip. We checked our bags in at reception, they offered to order us a taxi which arrived promptly. Nerves were really starting to get the better of me during the cab ride. Whitney squeezed my hand every few minutes offering her support as best she could. I was going out on a whim arriving at an address I wasn't even sure she lived at anymore, I had no way of contacting her other than the scrap of paper, that contained the scribbled first line of her address and area code.

The house wasn't quite what I expected, it was somewhere I could imagine living myself, beautifully painted a dark red, with a fresh white porch, the windows and doors were also white. The number read 42 in big silver numerals, this was the place. There was only a small garden to the front, with a driveway and garage to the left. I knew the main features would be to the rear of the property, with it being a beach house the views were bound to be immense. The house looked very well looked after, like most property's on the street, a fresh new hanging basket lay to the right of the door, with several plant pots to the left, leading up and onto the porch where a small chair sat still in the windless air. It was picturesque, the perfect postcard for what seemed like the perfect little coastal town. There was no car parked in the driveway, no windows open or doors ajar, no sign of any life inside the house.

"Go on, go and knock. I'll wait here." Whitney nudged me towards the steps slamming me back into reality. Three consecutive raps on the door was all it took to realise that nobody was coming to open it. The piercing doorbell was loud enough to alert anyone within the vicinity that somebody was at the door.

"Maybe she's out back? Or down at the beach?" Whitney was clutching at anything she could for my sake. I think she hoped just as much as I did that Alex was there.

"Let's take a look."

The back of the house was as I expected, the view of the beach, sea and surrounding coastal towns made it the perfect holiday home. In that moment I could see why Rose wanted to go there, this place was held dear to her heart, many a time she had spent her summers there, with her husband and her children and eventually her grandchildren. It was a walk down memory lane for Rose, a time to remember everything her life had been and had become. What better way to leave this life than in a place where you truly lived it, a place where you could be at peace with the world, knowing that on the other side you would be reunited with the people that made that place so special. I saw the appeal instantly, I hoped one day, I too would have a place like cannon beach.

"Anything down there Whit?" I shouted.

I had peered through every window, the inside looked so cosy and warm, the brick walls had been accompanied by a beautiful, soft, leather, brown couch. Stacks of wood displayed neatly at the side of the fire. The interior was unusual for a beach house, it was almost like taking the inside of a cabin somewhere, maybe out in the cold depths of Alaska, and placing it right there in the sunny beach side resort. Unusual, yet beautiful.

"Nothing Kacy, any luck up here?"

"No there's no sign of anyone inside, the house looks so neat and tidy through the windows. I'm starting to worry that maybe she isn't staying here anymore." I'm certain that Whitney could see the pain that was now quite apparent, across my face. I tried my best to hide it.

"Maybe we should have a closer look, surely there's a key somewhere around here……." Whitney rummaged underneath each plant pot, one after the other, "….everyone leaves a spare key outside or is that just in the movies." She continued to rummage, but came up with nothing.

"I guess were not in the movies then, it would certainly be easier than this." She let out a loud sigh in unison with my own.

"Now what?" were the only words I could manifest, chosen from an overwhelming swarm of thoughts clouding my head.

"Do you think it's a sign? Maybe someone is telling me it's time to move on, that I shouldn't dredge up the past anymore. Why didn't I ask her for her number before she left, then there would be none of this hassle. I was just so certain she would come back last night. Do you think I was naive? Hoping for too much by coming here?" I sat myself down on the porch steps, completely hopeless.

"I think you need to stop blaming yourself, you followed your heart and you did what you felt you needed to do.

There are people out there that would have moved on, they wouldn't have taken a chance like you did, and those people will live to regret it for the rest of their lives, but you honey, you will be able to tell yourself that you didn't give up. Who says it's over anyway? You are 21 years old nearly 22, you have the rest of your life ahead of you. I believe Alex will walk back into it at some point, even if that's not today." I smiled my best smile at my very best friend, she really was the one person in my life that I knew would always know what to say. Words were beyond me at that moment, I lay on Whitney's shoulder until the hurt subsided.

"Why don't you leave her a note? Then when she comes back she has a way of contacting you? Even if she doesn't happen to live here anymore, you can only try right?" she had a point, what was the harm in trying. "Okay good idea, I'll do it now. I'm sure I have some paper in here somewhere." I routed through my rather large satchel bag, amongst a book, some sweets and my headphones, was my diary which had several pieces of unused paper at the back, I quickly began to scroll down a few words.

Alex,

I don't know what happened last night, you didn't come back so I came to your house, at least I think this is still your house. You weren't here so I had no other choice, but to leave and head back to Raleigh. I just want you to know that I looked for you, I didn't just leave. I have missed you so much over the past few months, you have no idea.

Last night just brought back a flood of memories, it made me realise just how in love with you I still am, and I think always will be. I'm so sorry things turned out the way they did, I'm sorry I didn't believe you, the first thing I seem to do is doubt people, I should of known better with you. I fly out at 17:30 pm today, if you come back in time and read this note I would love to see you before I go. I need to see you. I love you Alex, I hope you still feel the same too. Goodbye for now my love.

Kacy

P.S. My new number is printed on the front of this letter, if I don't hear from you then I guess it just wasn't meant to be.

I carefully tore out the small piece of paper, folding it three ways before I posted it through the antique looking, black letter box. My last hope and my last resort written upon a scrap of paper. I hoped it would find its way to Alex knowing that if it didn't, I was all out of options.

"There it's done, I need a drink."

"Little early for alcoholic beverages I think K, maybe a coffee." We both laughed and smiled at one another, I don't think I could've stomached an alcoholic drink.

"Coffee sounds perfect."

CHAPTER TWELVE

"Jennifer you need to leave me alone now, I've heard everything you've had to say, you're just repeating everything you said last night. I don't want to hear it so please, just leave." Alex fiddled in her pocket for her house keys, she needed to get away from the constant screeching sound of Jennifer trying to worm her way out of the situation.

"No Alex I'm not leaving until you admit that you love me, that your feelings for me are real, don't make out like what I did was an awful thing, I did it because I wanted you, because I knew we had something between us." Jennifer pushed her way through the front door behind Alex into a home she had made herself more than comfortable in, over the past few months.

"You broke up me and my girlfriend, you had no right to interfere with my personal life Jennifer, you saw how heartbroken I was after we split up and you just stood there knowing full well that you were the cause, how could you even do that? I don't know you anymore, I thought you were a sweet girl, so kind and innocent, clearly I was wrong."

"Alex just admit that you love me, we can make this work, I know we can. I did it all for us, all I want is to make you happy."

"I do not love you Jennifer, I've never loved you, yes I liked you, but that was all fake. You made me feel that way because you poisoned my head with thoughts of Kacy cheating on me and not wanting me anymore, you made me feel like I needed you, when it was all a lie, I never loved you!!!" the words may have seemed harsh, but justified giving the circumstances, she meant every word.

Alex's voice rose with every syllable to really drive home the point. She left Jennifer stood in the living room and went straight to the fridge to pore herself a drink, she had spent all night arguing with her, more than once she had wanted to leave, but Jennifer had latched onto her body and forced her to stay and hear her out at least. All she wanted was to go and see Kacy, she thought she'd gotten away that morning, only to realise Jennifer was following her back in the car, she certainly wasn't giving up without a fight. Alex made her way back into the living room to catch Jennifer reading a small scrap of paper, she wondered why she had all of a sudden gone quiet.

"What are you reading?"

"Nothing much, just something I had in my pocket."

Jennifer looked alarmed, Alex could sense she was lying, she had noticed a small piece of paper on the floor in amongst the day's post, but hadn't felt the need to bend down and pick it up immediately, she then noticed that the same piece of paper was funnily enough gone.

"Give it to me Jennifer, I know you picked it up from my post."

"What is it with her Alex? Why is she so much better than me? Huh? Your perfect little Kacy, can't do a thing wrong can she?"

"Kacy is the love of my life Jennifer, she has been since the moment I laid eyes on her and she will be for the rest of my life, why can't you grasp that? I'm sorry but I am not the person for you, you might think I am right now, but you will find someone else who loves you for you. You can't honestly believe that a relationship can blossom and last when it starts in a dishonest way. Please Jennifer, I don't want to argue with you anymore, I don't want to hear any more excuses I just want you to give me that piece of paper and leave." That was when Jennifer ripped the letter into tiny pieces, throwing them onto the hard wood floor at Alex's feet.

"Here, there's your letter, when you realise that you got it wrong you know where you can find me."

"Don't hold your breath Jennifer, thanks for making this such an easy decision." She shouted after her as Jennifer stormed down the steps and sped away in her beaten up Volvo.

For the next ten minutes Alex tried her best to get some message from the crumpled pieces of paper that now lay upon the kitchen table. All she could seem to string together were a few sentences, "I don't know what happened...........you weren't here so I had no other choice..........I love you................I'm sorry I didn't believe you.........P.S. my number is printed....." where was her number printed? Alex searched frantically through the pieces of paper, but couldn't see any numbers, not even one. No matter which ways she put the pieces back together it just wasn't adding up, it was as if a piece or even two were missing. She had already double checked the floor in the living room several times, rearranging pieces of furniture to check it hadn't slid underneath. Still no sign of any remaining pieces. Alex slumped down onto the living room chair, totally and utterly defeated. The day had flown by it was almost 16:30 pm, she had already called the hotel on the way back from Jennifer's house, the clerk on reception had insisted the two young girls staying in room 34 had in fact checked out an hour earlier. Maybe if she left right now she could catch Kacy at the airport before she left, but the airport was 30 minutes away maybe even 45 with traffic, she had no idea of her flight time, and maybe she had already left.

What now? That was the ultimate question on Alex's mind, what did she have here in Oregon now? Sadly her grandma had passed, she was still utterly heartbroken, but her sister had flown back to Raleigh last week to restart her life there, she insisted on taking charge of the bar again and trying her best to get back to normal. Alex missed her sister, she missed her friends, and most importantly she missed Kacy. Raleigh was her life, it always had been. She knew what she had to do.

CHAPTER THIRTEEN

It was almost 17:00 pm, we had been at the airport for the past two hours and would shortly begin to board. We had spent the whole afternoon drinking coffee and browsing the boutiques in town much to Whitney's delight she finally bought the 'dress of her dreams' as she called it. My mind had been completely pre-occupied throughout the whole experience, wondering where Alex was, what she was doing, did she see my letter? The thoughts were nonstop, sometimes I prayed to turn them off, to just take away all the emotions I felt at that moment. If only I could've just flicked a switch so all the pain would go away, but this wasn't some episode of The Vampire Diaries and I wasn't a vampire so I guess that was out of the question.

"I guess she's not coming then."

At that point I don't think my heart could have broken any more than it already was.

"I don't think it's because she doesn't want to Kacy, maybe she hasn't seen the letter? She loves you Kacy it's so obvious don't ever forget that, keep the faith babe. It will all work out the way it's supposed to."

"Yeah, maybe you're right. I mean it can't exactly get any worse can it?" I spoke too soon, a text appeared on my phone from an unknown number, it was Alex and my heart did break just that little bit more.

From: Unknown

Kacy,
I'll only say this once. Please leave now and never look back. I couldn't come to the airport. It just wasn't necessary. I spent all night and day with Jennifer to realise that she is the one I want now. I believe too much has happened between me and you to ever go back. I loved you once Kacy, but those feelings are no more. If it helps you to move on then please hate me, I deserve that. I wish you the best in everything you do in the future, I hope you find the right person for you, like I found Jennifer. You'll never hear from me again and I hope you can refrain from contacting me too, I think it would be best for us both. Take care.
Alex

I couldn't breathe, why was she saying those things to me now, after the hopeful words she had spoken last night? Had Jennifer gotten to her, made her believe she was in fact the one she wanted? I hated Jennifer. The one emotion that rose above every other was my hate for that woman, how dare she ruin my relationship, she can't get the girl, she was the bad person in all of it, surely she wouldn't win. That's not how it was supposed to go. Whitney could see my eyes glaze over, she saw my knees go weak at the thought of losing Alex forever. I couldn't bring myself to speak a word, so many thoughts clouded my head, but I couldn't even spring a sentence together. I passed my phone over so she could see for herself.

The airport intercom bellowed out, bringing me out of a trance "All passengers flying on the AR88446 flight to Raleigh, your gate is now ready for boarding".

I couldn't bring myself to stand, any normal bodily function seemed like the hardest of tasks. I now knew what it felt like to truly break down, it had all become too much for me to handle. The ups and downs over the past few months had been some of the worst I'd ever experienced, it had right then gotten to the point were I couldn't take it anymore. I had given my all, I had loved her with everything in me and now I was lost amongst a sea of people, I was truly lost.

"Come on honey, let's get out of here. It's going to be okay, I promise you." Whitney wrapped a tight arm around my waist and led me to the gate, how it would ever be okay I didn't know.

"Thank you for being here for me Whit, I love you."
"Always sweetie, that's what best friends are for is it not? I love you too."

The next day work felt like such a traumatic experience. I loved my work, some days I honestly couldn't wait to get there, it meant I could begin my latest project, but all the energy and enthusiasm I had for anything had disappeared. The night before had gone as best it could, we had arrived back home at 23:30 pm, so both my parents and my brother were in bed. The thought of having to explain what had happened to them was unbearable. I snuck out the next morning earlier than usual, knowing my dad would still be sleeping and my mum would be starting her usual morning routine of exercise, shower, hair and makeup as well as making breakfast for everyone.

As soon as I heard her switch the shower on, it was my cue to leave. The drive to work had been slow, traffic was very light at 7 in the morning, I wasn't supposed to start work until 9 am, so I stopped for a coffee along the way hoping it would somehow wake me up. The night's sleep hadn't exactly been fulfilling, I spent most of the night crying and every time I managed to fall asleep the nightmares soon woke me back up. Lucky for me I had some of the best Chanel make-up available, the least I could do was try and cover up my puffy eyes, accompanied by the bulbous red tip of my nose.

After spending an extra twenty minutes on my face I looked somewhat presentable, I had gotten the scale from crying all night to absolutely hung over to slightly tired, not bad I thought to myself although I'm sure the mirror disagreed. The radio happened to be playing the most romantic songs of all time, no matter which station I changed to, I couldn't seem to get away from the heart wrenching love songs that I had once enjoyed. I eventually opted for silence and the sound of the road beneath me.

I had always been the happy, polite girl at work, I had often been called the life and soul of the business, always opting to arrange staff birthdays at work, always doing the coffee runs during a long shift and taking my time to get to know each person individually, because I knew that the bonds you make at work give you a sense of belonging. I always thought it was better to be that way, to be the one that always said yes and never no, but sometimes it gets to be too much. I was slowly going crazy, all day I had the usual "Hey, how was your weekend?" "Hey Kacy, are you well?" on any given day I would reply to those comments at least fifteen times, I myself would be intrigued to find out how their weekend had been, but today I was not okay. I was the furthest thing from okay.

I went almost the whole day before the cracks started to show. I prayed right then that I wouldn't fall apart, not there, not in front of all my professional peers. I sat at my desk with a tissue in hand, swiping away tear after tear as they fell hoping that no one else could see. I didn't want to be the girl that brought her personal life to work, I didn't want pity or anyone to feel awkward at my expense. Just as I thought I'd caught the last tear, Diane Hardy walked into my office. Diane was an architect with similar credentials to my father, she had been in the business a long time, although it hadn't changed her appearance in the slightest, still rocking the same 80's hairstyle, the same pinstripe suit and small rectangular glasses that sat neatly at the end of her rather long nose. I had to give her credit, she really didn't care what other people thought, she had heard the jokes people would make over and over, but she kept her head high as if nothing bothered her, she came to work, she did her job and then hurried off home to her 'wonderful' husband and two children as she often described them.

I admired Diane, after fifteen long years of service I guess you could say she was pretty much part of the building itself. Diane Hardy lingered at the door for what felt like an eternity, clearly she must have been weighing up the options, whether to turn and leave as if she'd gotten the wrong office or whether to offer comforting words of advice. Diane being the lovely woman she was opted for the latter.

"Hi there Kacy, are you okay sweetie? Sorry to barge in on you like this, it seems to me like you want to be alone right now. Should I come back?" her voice was so sweet and tentative, I could imagine her being some form of therapist.

"Hi Diane, no it's fine, I'll be okay. Can I help you with something?"

"I was just hoping you could show me how to work the new IOS system on my office computer, I can't seem to get my head around it and I know you young kids are all about technology these days. It's no rush though, whenever you're free would be great." Her smile was genuine and considerate. I'm sure she felt awful for asking a favour at a time when she could see I was upset, so I quickly reassured her that it wasn't a problem at all, I would be up to have a look as soon as I'd finished my latest presentation.

"Can I ask something Kacy?"

"Sure go ahead."

"If the reason you are upset is because of a boy…..or girl, I know how you young kids like to try it both ways. Then please I have a few words of advice for you." I almost laughed at the statement she was trying to make, she was probably the only person I worked with that didn't know I was a Lesbian, then again older woman liked to think we were all just experimenting, kind of like my grandma. We didn't see her often, but she certainly didn't like to admit that her granddaughter liked woman and not men, she would often become embarrassed if the subject was ever breeched, but I soon learned to live with that.

"You my dear are a beautiful young lady, one day when the person discovers just how much you loved them, they will soon realise that bright stars like you don't wait around, your brightness cannot be hidden under clouds for too long, you need to break free and shine to your full potential. Make sure you are loved by someone who loves you for you and would never see those tears fall from your eyes, because my dear starting today you need to forget what has gone, appreciate everything you still have and most definitely look forward to all the amazing things, that will undoubtedly come. You are young, your life is just beginning and those tears you cry right now will only make you stronger, I have lived long enough to know this." I stood from behind my desk, I said nothing instead I embraced her with open arms, a hug was the only thing I could fathom in that moment. This woman I hardly knew, had taken the time to give me powerful words of inspiration, she had no idea what I was going through, but she did it anyway. I wished right then that there was more people in the world like Diane Hardy.

"Thank you so much Diane, I appreciate the words of wisdom."

"That's alright my dear, you know where I am if you ever need some more, I've been on this planet for 58 years I guess you could say I have enough knowledge to last another 58 years. I am more than happy to share it with you, anytime you wish." I didn't know who I could compare Diane Hardy to, you always expected your grandparents to know a lot about life. Diane was a lot younger than my grandparents yet the wisdom in her eyes and the way she spoke, made it seem like she had been around for centuries.

I later found out that she had been a school teacher for ten years before becoming an author, publishing several high rated novels before she eventually studied to be an architect. I made it my aim to get to know Diane some more, after all her words had cheered me up in a way that no one else had been able to.

The rest of the day went rather quickly, I had decided not to dwell on my personal life at work, what good would it do? I needed to keep my mind occupied by any means necessary, so that's exactly what I did. I arrived home a little after 6 pm, I was due to finish at 5 pm, but I always found myself to be one of the last ones out. Always trying to get a step ahead for the next day, several people had told me that the big boss himself Mr Graham Ranger, was noticing my eagerness to work and put in the hours, which certainly looked good on me. The one thing I had been dreading on the ride home was confronting my parents, dodging them in the morning had been rather easy, but I wasn't about to get away tonight as well, it was time to tell them everything. The house was rather silent when I entered, unusual for a Monday evening, Jason always had his friends over for a pizza and PlayStation night after football practice, but for some reason there was no obnoxious boys running through the house or wolf whistling at me as I walked through the door, so I figured maybe it had been cancelled.

"Kacy, honey is that you?" the angelic voice only usually came out when she wanted something.

"Yes mom, 2 seconds." I hung my coat up and kicked off my shoes in the usual place, I put on my best happy face and made my way through to the kitchen, dad was too enthralled in the football on television to even realise I had entered the house, my mother on the other hand was more than eager to embrace me before I even had chance to dump my bag on the worktop.

"So, how was work? I imagine you must be in a great mood after the weekend's antics?" Not quite, if she only knew. It certainly wasn't going to be easy running through everything in my head again, but she had to know.

"Work was okay mum, the usual really. Listen there's something I need to tell you."

"If it's about Alex stopping over here that isn't a

problem, you two are a couple and its more than fine by me. You know I have no problem with her now that the two of you have worked out your differences, we had a good talk about it earlier today anyway."

"Wait, what? Had a talk with who?"

"Well Alex of course silly, don't get upset though I didn't broach the whole subject, I played it cool as if nothing had happened. I knew you wouldn't want me to discuss your relationship without you being there." She had to be kidding me, I think my mum was losing the plot.

"Alex was here? This afternoon? Like right here in our house?"

"Yes Alex, you know the one you flew to Oregon for? Are you feeling okay sweetie?"

"Yes I......erm.......I'm just a little shocked is all....did she say anything?"

"She told me to give you this piece of paper, don't worry I haven't read it, why you kids can't just call each other up or text these days I'll never know, although the writing romantic letters is rather Romeo and Juliet don't you think?" I was staring at my mother, then at the piece of paper in her hand totally unresponsive to anything she had said, nothing registered since she confirmed that Alex had in fact been in our home that day.

"Uh..Huh....anyway mum I've got....to.....erm....go." with that I flung my bag from the counter over my shoulder and headed for the stairs and the safety of my bedroom.

"Wait honey what do you want for…….." I didn't catch the last bit. I imagine it had something to do with dinner, she was always talking about dinner until she was fully satisfied that I'd eaten. I threw my bag on the floor and carefully took a seat on the edge of my bed, the suspense was killing me. I felt a sudden sense of Deja vu, many a time I had sat in that same position building myself up to read one of Alex's letters, most of them were great, until the end when the thought of opening another letter filled me with a sudden surge of pain. This one was short and sweet.

Kacy,

I couldn't make sense of your letter that you left, Jennifer ripped it into pieces before I even got chance to read it. All I know is that I had to come back for you, there was nothing left for me in Oregon, my life is with you here in Raleigh. If you'll still have me that is. There is so much we need to talk about and so much I need to explain. I didn't get your number from the piece of paper you left, I'm not sure what happened to it, but I'll come back around 8'o clock this evening. I love you Kacy, I always have. Alex

It was almost 19:30, Alex would be here in half an hour. I quickly ran to the shower, in less than fifteen minutes I was back out with my hair thrown up in a messy ponytail, a slight tinted moisturiser applied to my face to give off a sun kissed, smooth skinned look. My clothes consisted of skinny jeans and a baggy top, my usual ensemble, not to girly and not to tomboyish. I didn't want to look ridiculously made up, like I had made some huge effort to look my best, but I also didn't want to be wearing the same work clothes I'd had on for the past twelve hours and the same smell of twelve hour old deodorant and faded perfume. I sprayed my latest perfume addition, Loverdose by Diesel. It was a smell I instantly fell in love with at the perfume shop, the woman had described it as 'a beautiful but deadly weapon of seduction' well that would certainly do the trick.

I eyed the bedside clock as it ticked over to 19:52, I suddenly had a few minutes to come to terms with the reality of it all. The ten minute shower had given me some alone time with my thoughts, I now had several new conclusions. The first being that Alex hadn't seen the letter or my phone number, which then I assumed that Jennifer must have and probably more than likely sent the nasty text I had received the day before. I would almost put my life on that being the truth. The second conclusion was that Alex still loved me, she said it right there in the letter, she had flown all the way back to Raleigh to be with me and to work things out, which took me to my third and final pressing thought, do I tell her about Lara?

There was a sudden pang of guilt when I thought or said her name out loud, I knew myself that I had done nothing wrong, me and Alex were broken up, besides she had been seeing Jennifer which kind of made things even, but the difference was Lara was now my friend, I didn't want to lose her. She had become a part of my life that I wasn't sure I could live without. I knew without a shadow of a doubt that I loved Alex, that she was the one I wanted to spend the rest of my life with, but Lara was someone I didn't want to compromise, the only way I could figure it all out would be to come clean, to tell Alex everything. Surely she would understand, at least that's what I hoped.

The doorbell rang taking me away from my many thoughts, to just the one. Alex.

CHAPTER FOURTEEN

There she stood, in the doorway to my bedroom, a silhouette of perfection. Almost so unreal to me that I had to make sure I wasn't dreaming. Neither of us knew what to say, who should speak first, I wasn't entirely sure. The silence was broken when Alex spoke.

"Kacy please forgive me for everything, I should have known you wouldn't just leave me, that you wouldn't cheat on me. I should've come back and fought for you. I'm so sorry that Jennifer came between us, but I'm here now if you'll still have me, I've come back for you and only you."

"I'm sorry too, I'm sorry that I didn't come sooner I didn't want to believe that you'd hurt me either, deep down I knew you wouldn't, but I guess when the evidence mounted up I was too heartbroken to try and believe otherwise. I never stopped loving you Alex. I'm so happy that you've come back. Please don't leave me again." right then I was the most vulnerable I'd ever been, I knew she could make me or break me, she was the type that stole your heart in an instant. One look, one touch and I was under her spell and no doubt forever would be.

We both eyed each other from across the room, words suddenly forgotten by the both of us.

I was taken aback by the rare beauty stood before me, I realised there and then just how incredibly sexy she really was. I just wanted to feel the touch of her lips upon mine, knowing I would instantly forget the entire world. I just needed her that was all, just her in that moment to make everything go back to the way it was supposed to be. I looked deep into her eyes, I saw her soul, bared open just for me. For the briefest of moments everything stood still, the anticipation of her lips on mine was so intense. I almost ran towards her with a sudden urge of desire racing through my veins. The kiss was overpowering, like nothing I had ever experienced. The taste of her lips, the way she pulled me in at the waist and held the back of my neck just below my hair filled me with an overwhelming passion for her. "Wait...are you sure?...don't you want to talk about..." I forced my lips back upon hers, "No more talking...not now."

We both felt the rawness and intensity in that moment, I looked deep into Alex's eyes, those gorgeous piercing blue eyes, I knew she could feel what I needed right now. I slowly closed the door behind her flicking the lock to the right as I dragged her by the hand towards the bed. I had never wanted anything as much in my whole life, piece after piece of clothing fell to the floor, first my top, her jacket, my jeans, her jeans, finally both our underwear fell to the floor and there was nothing left, but the softness of her entirely naked body lying over mine.

We had always made love in the past, but this was so different, this was a ferocious need for one another, an incredible overpowering desire to feel her body upon mine, to feel her lips caressing every inch of my naked figure. The feeling was incredible, I wrapped my legs around Alex's bare waist as she lifted me up and caressed my neck, slowly moving all the way down my back with such delicate touches. She pulled away and looked deep into my eyes,

"I love you Kacy. I never stopped loving you."

My heart ached for her, I ached to take away the guilt I could see hidden behind her words. Guilt that wasn't hers to feel. I would show her that none of this was her fault, I would show her just how much I really loved her, more than words could ever explain.

"I love you too Alex. I always will."

We lay side by side for a while, so close and so complete now that we had each other again. Each kiss afterwards brought a wave of ecstasy. If that moment was the last I ever lived in, I would happily take that. If she was the last person I ever laid with, the last person I ever kissed or made love too then my life would have been the greatest of all lives, because she was it for me, she was the definition of true love. I now knew what it felt like to love someone beyond believe.

Alex wiped the hair from my eyes, I assumed so she could look straight at them with a stare that blocked out the world around us.

"What? What are you thinking?"

"I'm thinking how lucky I am to be led next to the most beautiful girl in the world. You really are the envy of all woman do you know that?"

"Don't be silly, you're just saying that because you just got lucky." I nudged her playfully in the ribs. It felt so good to be by her side, to hear her laughter like no time had passed.

"No I mean it, in all seriousness. I should have never let you go so easily Kacy, I was just so hurt and with everything that happened with my grandma. I guess I'm just so happy that we found each other again. I don't ever want to be without you." a small tear formed in the corner of my eye as I saw just how meaningful every word was. I was yet to ask her about how Rose died or when she died. I just hoped that it was peaceful, she had been an amazing woman who brought so much light to the lives of the people who knew her. I knew there would be a void in Alex now, a void that nothing would ever fill.

"You will never have to be, I promise."

"Marry me?"

"Huh..." was that aimed at me or was I missing something?

"I know it might sound crazy but the moment I met you I knew my life would never be the same. I am not the person I want to be without you, you make my life complete, you make everything worth it. I know that the past few months have been hard, I know that we have only known each other eleven months, but you are it for me Kacy, I know it with every inch of my heart. Rose told me that the moment I knew I couldn't live without someone was the moment I needed to make them mine forever, I can't live without you Kacy. So please, I promise to you, right here, right now that if you say yes I will spend the rest of my life making you happy. Will you marry me?"

I wanted nothing more than to spend the rest of my life with her, the shock was momentarily paralyzing not because I didn't want to marry her, but because I didn't expect to be proposed to by this amazing woman. Yesterday I was single, I was heartbroken and now the love of my life was asking to marry me, I guess you could say it was certainly a turnaround of events. My life had gone from an utter disaster to the most amazing life I could have ever asked for, all because of Alex. There was no other answer that would slip from my lips other than the one I truly meant. The one that would start my life with the woman I loved right then, a life and a love I could have only dreamed of. With that being said I seized the day.

"Yes. Of course I'll marry you.

TWO YEARS LATER

"Lara you made it." I was so delighted to see my best friend, it had been a month since she left Raleigh to travel around America.

"Well I just had to come back, I couldn't wait to see your new pad, and it looks amazing." I gave her a huge hug.

"It's so good to see you, I hope you'll be working back at the bar soon, I know Alex misses you."

"I sure will, I won't be able to afford the rent in that apartment otherwise, how you got Alex to let me have it that cheap, I'll never know. I owe you one K."

"What are best friends for? All the guys are through in the lounge, it was supposed to be a low key house warming party, let's just say half the town seems to have turned up." She laughed as she put her arm around my shoulder.

"I've missed you so much, travelling the country isn't fun without my partner in crime. Is Whitney here? I'd like to see her face in person, instead of the blurred version on Skype."

"She sure is, go ahead and sit down, I'll get you a drink. Vodka and lemonade?"

"You know it babe." She winked.

I was in the best place I could be, surrounded by my best friends and the woman I loved.

Life was perfect.

Printed in Great Britain
by Amazon

71210519R00108